GCSE English

Macbeth

by William Shakespeare

Studying English texts can give you a real headache,
but happily this CGP book makes your life just a little bit easier.

This book has everything you need to write a brilliant essay about *Macbeth*.
It doesn't just tell you what happens — it's got analysis of the main characters,
themes, historical background and language features too.

Plus, there are plenty of practice questions and a worked exam answer
with tips on how to improve your grade on the big day.

And of course, we've done our best to make the whole
experience at least vaguely entertaining for you.

The Text Guide

Contents

Introduction

Section One — Understanding Shakespeare

Section Two — Discussion of Acts

Section Three — Characters

Contents

Section Four — Context and Themes

Section Five — Shakespeare's Techniques

Section Six — Assessment Advice

Published by CGP

Editors:
Claire Boulter
Holly Corfield-Carr
Heather Gregson
Holly Poynton
Caley Simpson

With thanks to Glenn Rogers and Nicola Woodfin for the proofreading.
With thanks to Laura Jakubowski and Laura Stoney for the copyright research.

Acknowledgements:

Cover Illustration: Glamis Castle (w/c on paper) by Girtin, Thomas (1775-1802) (attr. to) Private Collection/ The Bridgeman Art Library.

Page 1: Macbeth and the Witches, 1793-94 (oil on canvas) by Fuseli, Henry (Füssli, Johann Heinrich) (1741-1825) Petworth House, Sussex, UK/ The Egremont Collection/ National Trust Photographic Library/Derrick E. Witty/ The Bridgeman Art Library.

With thanks to iStockphoto.com for permission to use the image on page 1.

Images on pages 3, 4, 5, 9, 11, 15, 17, 18, 19, 21, 27, 28, 30, 31, 33, 39, 41, 44, 52, 55 and 57 taken of the Macbeth Production of the Department of Theatre and Dance, College of Fine Arts, The University of Texas, Austin, USA. Directed by Ken Albers, Costume Design: Candida Nichols, Set Design: David Utley, Lighting Design: Monique Norman, Photographer: Amitava Sarkar.

Images on pages 3, 10, 34, 40, 43 and 54 from the Shakespeare's Globe Theatre production of Macbeth, photographer Ellie Kurtz.

Images on pages 3, 6, 8, 13, 20, 22, 29, 35, 38, 42 and 47 © COLUMBIA / THE KOBAL COLLECTION.

Image on page 7 © CROMWELL / LAMANCHA / GRAMPIAN TV / THE KOBAL COLLECTION.

Image on page 32 © BRITISH LION / THE KOBAL COLLECTION.

Image on page 48 © BRITISH LION / THE KOBAL COLLECTION / BOULTON, DAVIS.

With thanks to Alamy for permission to use the images on pages 2, 5, 12, 14, 23 and 26.

With thanks to Rex Features for permission to use the images on pages 16 and 51.

ISBN: 978 1 84146 116 8

Website: www.cgpbooks.co.uk

Printed by Elanders Ltd, Newcastle upon Tyne.

Clipart from CorelDRAW®

Based on the classic CGP style created by Richard Parsons.

Introduction to 'Macbeth' and Shakespeare

'Macbeth' is about the **Corrupting Power** of **Ambition**

- *Macbeth* is about an ambitious nobleman who murders the Scottish King after some Witches make a prediction that he will rule Scotland.
- Macbeth becomes a cruel king who commits many crimes, before he is eventually killed.
- *Macbeth* is one of Shakespeare's most-performed plays. Its themes of ambition and betrayal are still relevant today, and the basic plot has inspired many adaptations.

Macbeth is about ambition and betrayal

1) Shakespeare shows that even honourable men can be corrupted by ambition — Macbeth betrays his king, his country and his own conscience to satisfy his lust for power.
2) Macbeth and Lady Macbeth show that power that's taken unfairly doesn't bring happiness, but leads to guilt, madness and death.

Macbeth meets the Witches.

Shakespeare is the most **Famous** writer in the English language

- William Shakespeare wrote at least thirty-seven plays and a lot of poems.
- He wrote some of the most famous plays in the English language, including comedies (such as *Twelfth Night*), tragedies (such as *Romeo and Juliet* and *Hamlet*) and histories (such as *Richard III*).
- *Macbeth* is one of his best-known tragedies.
- It was written in the 1600s, but the story is very loosely based on history — a man called Macbeth was King of Scotland in the 11th century.

1564	Born in Stratford-upon-Avon, Warwickshire.
1582	Married Anne Hathaway.
1583-85	Had three children — Susanna, Hamnet and Judith.
1585-92	Began an acting career in London.
1589-1613	Wrote most of his plays.
1611	First known performance of 'Macbeth'.
1616	Died, aged 52.

Background Information

'Macbeth' is set in various parts of **Scotland**

Here's a plan of the important places in the play, showing where all the important action happens.

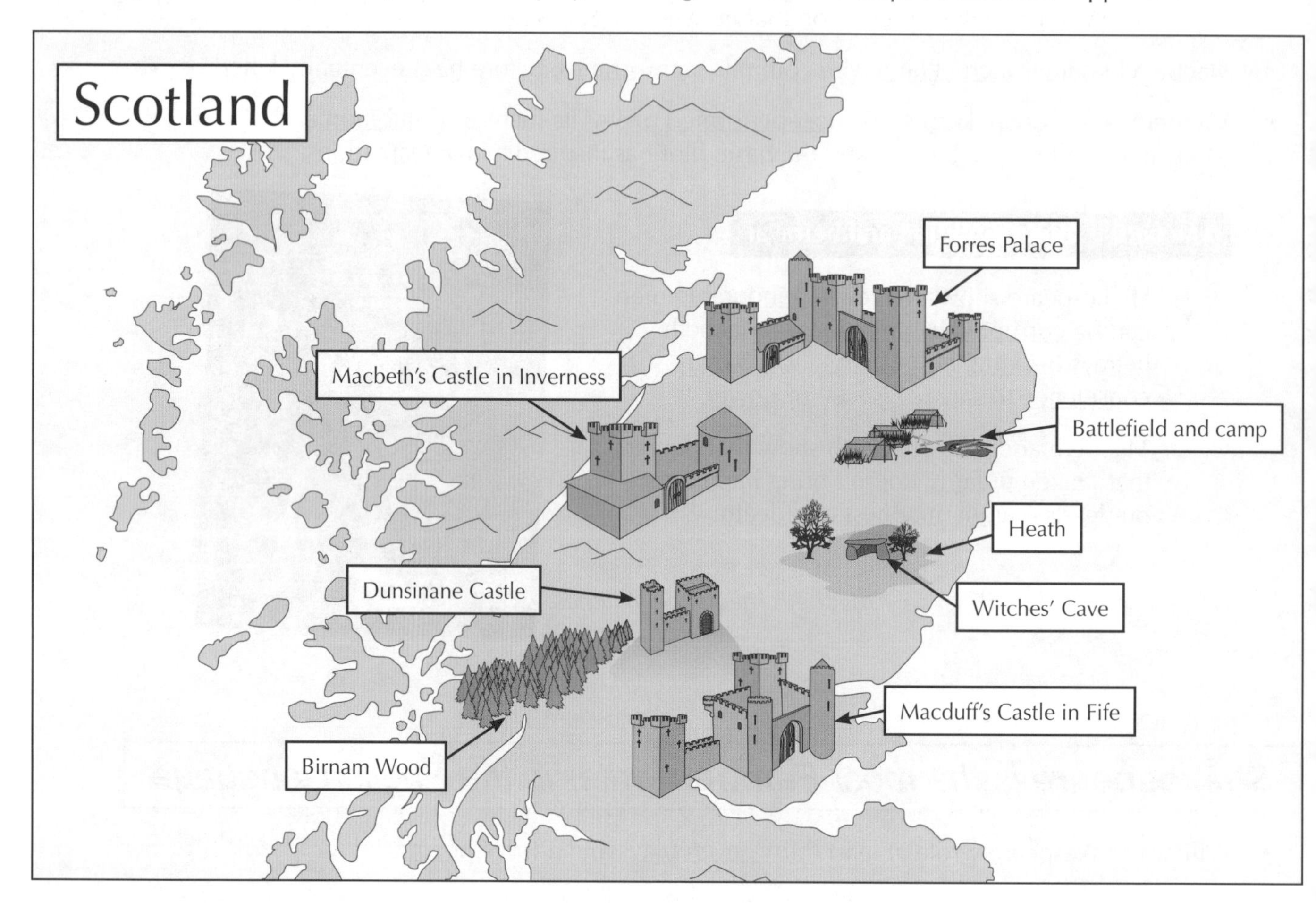

Theatre *was an important form of* ***Entertainment***

The rebuilt Globe Theatre in London.

- There was no TV, radio or internet in Shakespeare's time, so going to the theatre was really popular.
- The theatre wasn't just for rich people — Shakespeare's audiences included servants and labourers. Audiences could get quite rowdy during performances.
- The poorer people in the audience stood in front of the stage — if it rained, they got wet. The richer people sat in the covered galleries above.
- Shakespeare's theatre company, the King's Men (previously called the Lord Chamberlain's Men), performed in the Globe Theatre in London. This was rebuilt in 1997.
- It was illegal for women to act, so the women's parts were played by young boys (even Lady Macbeth...).

Who's Who in 'Macbeth'

Macbeth...

... is an ambitious Scottish nobleman. He murders the King of Scotland and takes his place.

Lady Macbeth...

... is Macbeth's wife. She persuades Macbeth to kill the King. She eventually goes mad and kills herself.

Duncan...

... is the King of Scotland at the start of the play. Macbeth murders him.

Malcolm...

... is Duncan's son. He flees after Duncan's murder, and becomes King at the end of the play.

Macduff...

... is a noble soldier. He doesn't trust Macbeth and eventually kills him.

Lady Macduff...

... is Macduff's wife. Macbeth has her and her children murdered.

Banquo...

... is a brave soldier and nobleman. He's friends with Macbeth but Macbeth has him killed.

Three Witches...

... are evil supernatural beings who can predict the future. Their leader is called Hecate.

'Macbeth' — Plot Summary

'Macbeth'... what happens when?

Macbeth needs to be as familiar to you as your favourite socks. This little recap of the main events will help you on your way, but it's no substitute for reading the play. There's no escaping that I'm afraid...

Act One** — The Witches make two **Prophecies

© Amitava Sarkar

- The three Witches plan to meet Macbeth.
- Macbeth and Banquo meet the Witches, who tell Macbeth he'll be Thane of Cawdor, then King. They tell Banquo his descendants will be kings.
- Duncan makes Macbeth Thane of Cawdor. Macbeth starts to wonder if the Witches' prophecy about him being King will come true too.
- Macbeth tells Lady Macbeth about the prophecy. She plans to persuade him to murder Duncan.
- Duncan comes to stay with the Macbeths. Macbeth is reluctant to kill him, but Lady Macbeth convinces him that they can frame Duncan's servants for the murder. Macbeth agrees to the plan.

***Acts Two and Three** — **Duncan** and **Banquo** bite the dust*

- Macbeth murders Duncan and Lady Macbeth plants blood-stained daggers on Duncan's servants.
- Macduff arrives and discovers the King's body. The King's sons, Malcolm and Donalbain, leave Scotland because they fear for their lives — this makes them look guilty of Duncan's murder.
- Rosse and an old man discuss the strange and unnatural things that have been happening since Duncan's murder. Macbeth is about to be crowned, but not all the other noblemen support him.
- Macbeth is now King, but he's worried by the Witches' prophecy about Banquo's descendants being kings. He orders some murderers to kill Banquo and his son, Fleance.
- The murderers kill Banquo, but Fleance escapes. Macbeth hosts a feast and sees Banquo's ghost. He decides to visit the Witches again.
- Lennox and a lord suspect Macbeth of murdering Duncan and Banquo. They say that Macduff is getting an army together to attack Macbeth and put Malcolm on the throne.

© Amitava Sarkar

Act Four — The Three Apparitions

© Amitava Sarkar

- Macbeth visits the Witches again and they summon three apparitions.
- Each apparition makes a prophecy. The first warns Macbeth about Macduff, the second tells him that no one born from a woman can harm him and the third tells him that he can't be beaten until Birnam Wood moves to Dunsinane Hill.
- When Macbeth demands to know if Banquo's children will ever rule Scotland the Witches show him Banquo's ghost and a line of kings who seem to be Banquo's descendants.
- Macduff has fled to England. Macbeth sends his murderers to kill Macduff's wife and children.
- In England, Macduff proves his loyalty to Malcolm, and Malcolm reveals that the English King has given him ten thousand soldiers to fight Macbeth. Macduff learns that Macbeth has killed his family, and vows to avenge their deaths.

Act Five — Macbeth is Overthrown

- Lady Macbeth has gone mad. She sleepwalks and keeps washing invisible blood from her hands.

© Amitava Sarkar

- The Scottish lords plan to meet the English army at Birnam Wood and attack Macbeth.
- Macbeth hears about the approaching English army. He isn't scared because of the Witches' predictions.
- Malcolm tells the soldiers to cut down branches from Birnam Wood and hide behind them as they march towards Macbeth's castle.
- Macbeth prepares for battle and finds out that Lady Macbeth has killed herself.
- Macbeth and Macduff meet on the battlefield. Macbeth is sure that he'll win, until he finds out that Macduff was born by Caesarean, so he isn't born from a woman. They fight and Macbeth is killed.
- Malcolm is made King of Scotland.

Macbeth? Macdeath more like...

Once you're confident that you know what happens in *Macbeth*, you're ready to start Section One. If you're still not sure about the plot or want a break from revision, have a look at the *Macbeth* cartoon at the back of the book.

© Lebrecht Music and Arts Photo Library / Alamy

How Plays Work

Lots of people think Shakespeare's the hardest thing you have to study for English — and they're right... but it should be less hard and less weird when you've read this section.

'Macbeth' is meant to be **Watched** — **Not** Read

1) *Macbeth* is a play. A play tells a story by showing it to you.
2) When you read the play, it's often pretty hard to follow what's going on. Try to imagine what's happening and how the people would speak and act — it should all start to make a lot more sense.
3) If you can, try to see the play on stage. If not, watch a film version to get an idea of the story.
4) But remember to read the play as well — films often cut scenes and change the language, so it's dangerous to rely on them too much.

'Macbeth' is a **Tragedy**

Macbeth is one of Shakespeare's most famous tragedies. Mostly, it's a typical tragedy...

1) It's about serious topics like war and death.
2) It's sad — lots of the characters die.
3) The play's main character (Macbeth) dies as a result of his flaws.

But there are also a few more unusual things...

4) There are supernatural elements — the three Witches and their prophecies.
5) Lady Macbeth isn't typical of Shakespeare's female characters — she's evil and strong-willed.
6) There are a few comic moments — the Porter is a comic character.

Pay Attention to the **Stage Directions**

When you're reading the play, look at the stage directions — they're little phrases in italics that tell the actors what to do, when to come in and when to leave the stage.

These are the really common stage directions in Shakespeare:

Enter = when someone comes onto the stage
Exit = when one person leaves the stage
Exeunt = when more than one person leaves
Aside = the character is talking to themselves, not to other characters on the stage

Tragedy — when the feeling's gone and you can't go on...

There's quite a lot of doom, gloom, revenge, death and war in *Macbeth* — but you do get some pretty cool witches thrown in for good measure. Lady Macbeth is a really interesting character too — a lot of Shakespearean women are a bit weak and pathetic, but she has balls. She's a bit nasty though, so perhaps not the best girl-power role model.

How to Understand Shakespeare's Language

Shakespeare's plays can be more confusing than a fox and ferret convention, especially all the strange ye olde language. But there are certain ways of reading it so it makes more sense...

The **Play** is written in **Poetry** and **Prose**

1) Some of the play is written in poetry — but the poetry doesn't always rhyme.
2) The poetry is the bits where all the lines are roughly the same length, and each line starts with a capital letter. It looks like this:

> "Still it cried, 'Sleep no more' to all the house,
> 'Glamis hath murdered sleep', and therefore Cawdor
> Shall sleep no more – Macbeth shall sleep no more."
> Act 2, Scene 2

3) The Witches, Hecate and the apparitions (the supernatural characters) speak in rhyming verse.
4) Some bits of the play are in prose — prose is normal sentences without any set rhythm.
5) Common characters, like the Porter, usually speak in prose. Lady Macbeth speaks in prose when she goes mad.

For more on poetry see Section 5.

Don't Stop Reading at the **End** of Each Line

1) Even though each line starts with a capital letter, it doesn't mean it's a separate sentence.
2) Just ignore the capitals and follow the punctuation.
3) For example, there's no full stop here so carry on to the next line:

> "My hands are of your colour, but I shame
> To wear a heart so white"
> Act 2, Scene 2

Look Out for **Words** in a **Funny Order**

1) Another reason Shakespeare can be tricky to understand is the long complicated sentences.
2) It's hard because the words are in a funny order. If you change the order it makes it easier to understand. For example:

> "So foul and fair a day I have not seen."
> Act 1, Scene 3

> I have not seen so foul and fair a day.

> "O, full of scorpions is my mind, dear wife!"
> Act 3, Scene 2

> O, my mind is full of scorpions, dear wife!

How to Understand Shakespeare's Language

Macbeth is full of cobwebby, dusty old words — and weird ways of writing things using apostrophes. Don't let them put you off — it *is* English really. I promise.

You have to ***Guess*** *what the* ***Missing Letters are***

1) Shakespeare often runs two words together and misses letters out to make them fit into a line.
2) There's often an apostrophe instead of the missing letter. So "is't" means "is it".

Act 4, Scene 1

What is't you do?

3) If you come across random apostrophes when you're reading, you'll have to work out what the missing letters are.

Mind Your ***Thees****,* ***Thous*** *and* ***Thys***

1) They had different words for 'you' in those days.
2) People used to say 'thou' to be familiar or friendly, and 'you' to be more formal. Look out for these words:

Thou	=	You
Thee	=	You
Thy	=	Your
Thine	=	Your

And finally, some more ***Old, Confusing Words***

1) Verbs often look a bit different from modern English...

thou art	=	you are	thou wilt	=	you will
thou hast	=	you have	thou canst	=	you can

2) If this seems difficult, here's a trick — take the 't' off the end of the verb:

hast – t = has

wilt – t = wil(l)

3) And here are a few more words to watch out for:

hie	=	go quickly	wherefore	=	why
hither	=	to here	thence	=	from there
whence	=	from where	ere	=	before
hence	=	from here	whither	=	where

For words funny order in a look out...

Right, so Shakespeare put his words in a funny order. It's very annoying and makes the plays difficult to read. But don't be too angry with him — he didn't start the trend. No. Go back further into history — in fact, you need to look to a long time ago, in a galaxy far, far away — then find someone else you will. Hmmm. May the Force be with you.

Analysis of Act One — The Witches and a Battle

This section goes over the story of *Macbeth*. Read it all and you'll know what happens in every scene. Don't go thinking you don't need to read the play as well, though. I'll find out if you don't.

Scene 1 — The Witches plan to Meet Macbeth

The wild weather hints that unnatural events are occurring.

1) The play starts with thunder and lightning, which sets a dark and violent mood.
2) The three Witches are the first characters on stage — this shows how important the theme of the supernatural is to the play. The Witches are mysterious — we don't know what their purpose is.
3) The Witches speak in rhyming couplets, e.g. "When the hurly-burly's done, / When the battle's lost and won." Only the supernatural characters in the play consistently use rhyme — it sets them apart from the other characters and makes their speech sound unnatural, as if they're casting an evil spell.
4) The Witches plan to meet Macbeth, but don't explain their intentions. Their final rhyming couplet, "Fair is foul, and foul is fair, / Hover through the fog and filthy air" hints that they're evil.

Theme — Reality and Appearances

The Witches introduce the idea that nothing is as it seems: "Fair is foul, and foul is fair". This theme is central to the play.

A paradox is a statement that contradicts itself.

Writer's Techniques — Language

The Witches speak in paradoxes — "When the battle's lost and won". At first they don't make any sense, but their predictions become clearer as the play goes on.

Scene 2 — King Duncan hears reports of the Battle

1) The Scottish army, led by Macbeth and Banquo, are fighting rebel armies from Norway and Ireland.
2) Shakespeare contrasts the eerie opening scene with the brutality and "bloody execution" of the battlefield. This sets a violent mood for the rest of the play.
3) The Captain and Duncan describe Macbeth as "brave" and "valiant". At this point he's a hero who's loyal to his king and country.

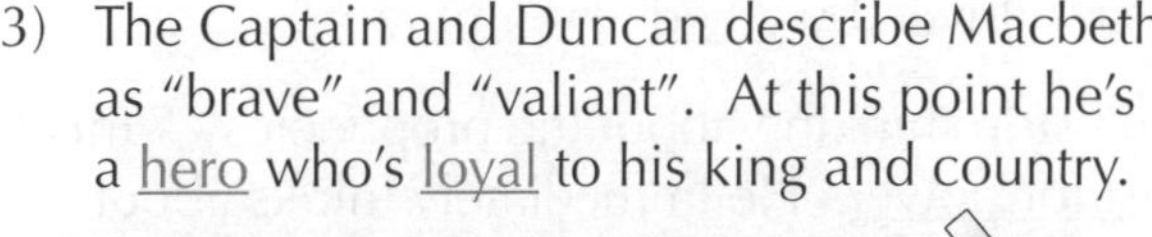

Character — Macbeth

At the start of the play Macbeth is celebrated for his bloodthirsty nature — he cut the traitor Macdonald "from the nave to the chops". It's ironic that this violence eventually leads to his downfall.

Theme — Reality and Appearances

The Witches have just told the audience that "Fair is foul" — this suggests that the "Worthy" Macbeth might not be as good as the other characters believe. The audience hasn't met Macbeth yet, so their view of him is based on what the other characters say.

Macbeth cuts off the traitor's head — this foreshadows (hints at something that happens later) his own death at the end.

Hugh Grant's latest film — 'Three Witches and a Battle'...

Macbeth starts as it means to go on — creepy witches that can see into the future, and bloody violence. Just in case you weren't already aware, The Scottish Play isn't a happy yarn about shortbread, tartan and the Loch Ness Monster.

Analysis of Act One — The Witches' Predictions

The Witches are back — and there's all sorts of hubble-bubble afoot.

Scene 3 — The Witches make **Three Predictions**

1) The Witches are accompanied by thunder again — this recurring motif hints at chaos, danger and the overturning of the natural order.

A motif is a recurring symbol — see pages 55 and 56.

2) Macbeth's first line in this scene, "So foul and fair a day I have not seen", immediately links him to the Witches and their "Foul is fair" prophecy.

Writer's Techniques — Metaphor

The Witches talk about sending a storm out on a sailor's ship so that he can't sleep. The sailor is a metaphor for what will happen to Macbeth, who's made sleepless by guilt, and the ship is a metaphor for Scotland, which is almost destroyed during Macbeth's violent reign.

Banquo and Macbeth **React Differently** to the Predictions

1) The Witches predict that Macbeth will be made Thane of Cawdor, then King, and that Banquo's descendants will also become kings. Banquo and Macbeth react differently to the news:

- Banquo is suspicious and questions his own sanity — he asks, "have we eaten on the insane root".
- He warns that the Witches "Win us with honest trifles — to betray's". He accepts that the Witches are telling the truth, but he's also aware that they're manipulating Macbeth and himself.
- Banquo's less easily deceived than Macbeth. He calls the Witches "instruments of darkness" because he sees they're evil, whereas Macbeth is less certain — he says they "Cannot be ill, cannot be good".
- The encounter with the Witches leaves Macbeth "rapt withal". He's spellbound by the predictions, but he's also scared by the powerful ambition that the Witches have awakened in him.

© Ellie Kurtz

2) The Witches tell Banquo he will be "Lesser than Macbeth, and greater". This is a reference to Banquo's sons being kings, but it could also mean that Banquo is greater because he isn't driven by greed and ambition.

3) Macbeth can't stop thinking about the prophecies — this shows his lust for power. He immediately thinks about killing Duncan, but he's also reluctant. At this point Macbeth isn't an evil character — he's wrestling with his conscience and torn between his ambition and his loyalty.

4) When Macbeth finds out he's been made Thane of Cawdor, it shows that the first prediction has come true. This convinces him that the prediction about him becoming King will come true too, which strengthens his ambition.

Character — The Witches

The Witches tell Banquo he will be "Not so happy, yet much happier". This hints that although Macbeth will get what he wants (he'll be King), it won't make him happy. The Witches use paradoxes and riddles to confuse Macbeth and Banquo and lead them astray.

The Weird sisters — the beard sisters more like...

The scene's set for a bit of action to take place. The Witches have told Macbeth that he'll be King, but Duncan and Malcolm stand in his way. Banquo's kids look like a threat to him too. So it looks like murder might be the answer...

Analysis of Act One — A Prediction Comes True

The next three scenes are all at Macbeth's castle — Macbeth and Lady Macbeth make their plan...

*Scene 4 — Macbeth is made **Thane of Cawdor***

Turning point in the action
The Witches' first prediction comes true.

1) Duncan gives Macbeth the title of Thane of Cawdor as a reward for his loyalty.

2) Duncan uses an extended metaphor of plants, e.g. "plant thee" and "make thee full of growing", to show that he sees it as his duty to nurture people who are loyal to him. Duncan sees Macbeth as a potential successor, suggesting that fate might make Macbeth King without him doing anything.

Theme — Kingship

Duncan is represented as a strong and fair leader — he rewards loyalty and wants Scotland to prosper. This contrasts with Macbeth's violent, tyrannical rule.

3) Macbeth seems confused in this scene. Outwardly he's a brave and loyal warlord, but inwardly his ambition is battling with his conscience. He wants to keep his "black and deep desires" hidden, not just from other people but from himself.

Theme — Reality and Appearances

Duncan says he misjudged the old Thane of Cawdor because there's no way to "find the mind's construction in the face" — he thinks that people who seem good and loyal may not be. It's ironic — he also misjudges Macbeth.

Writer's Techniques — Symbolism

Duncan says, "signs of nobleness, like stars, shall shine / On all deservers." He thinks that fate will reward those who deserve it. Light is also linked to visibility, which contrasts with Macbeth's desire to hide his intentions.

*Scene 5 — Lady Macbeth decides Duncan must **Die***

1) The scene opens with Lady Macbeth alone, reading a letter from Macbeth about the Witches' prophecies — this allows the audience to hear her inner thoughts and see what she's really like.

2) She has no doubts about killing Duncan and immediately sees that she'll have to force Macbeth to do it because he's "too full o'th'milk of human kindness".

3) Lady Macbeth's soliloquy uses evil imagery such as "smoke of hell" and "direst cruelty", which shows the evil on her mind.

© Amitava Sarkar

Writer's Techniques — Symbolism

Lady Macbeth asks the spirits to "unsex me here" — she doesn't want to be a woman because she sees women as weak and incapable of murder. For more on the symbolism of masculinity have a look at p.57.

4) Her speech links her to the Witches — she uses imperatives, which make it sound like she's casting a spell. She says, "Come, you spirits" and "Come, thick night", which links her to evil, unnatural spirits.

5) Macbeth enters and their dialogue in lines 56-58 is in half-line breaks. This makes their speech sound urgent and hurried — they're both nervous and need to act quickly in case they're interrupted.

There's more bloodshed afoot — Thane old, Thane old...

So Macbeth is the King's BFF and has just got a nice shiny new castle, but he still wants more — what a greedy guts. I bet Macbeth's the type to eat so much haggis at an all-you-can-eat buffet that he has indigestion for days afterwards.

Analysis of Act One — The Macbeths Plot to Kill

Duncan arrives at Macbeth's castle — he's in for the night of his life...

Scene 6 — Duncan and the Lords ***Arrive*** *at* ***Macbeth's Castle***

1) Duncan arrives at Macbeth's castle and is grateful for his hospitality and everything Macbeth's done for him.
2) Lady Macbeth appears to be the perfect hostess — she flatters Duncan and thanks him for the "honours deep and broad" he has given them. Shakespeare contrasts this scene with the previous one to show how false Lady Macbeth is.

Writer's Techniques — Irony

Duncan describes Macbeth's castle as "pleasant" and says that it "sweetly recommends itself". It's ironic that Duncan feels happy and welcome at Macbeth's castle — the audience knows what Macbeth's got planned.

Writer's Techniques — Irony

Duncan describes Macbeth's love for Lady Macbeth as "sharp as his spur". This is ironic — it wasn't love that made Macbeth rush home but his desire to plot Duncan's murder with Lady Macbeth. It's also ironic because Lady Macbeth is the spur (encouragement) that drives Macbeth into action.

Scene 7 — The Macbeths agree to ***Kill*** *Duncan*

© AF archive / Alamy

1) Scene 7 opens with Macbeth's soliloquy — he's trying to decide whether to kill Duncan and gives a list of reasons why he shouldn't:
   - He knows that murder can "return / To plague th'inventor", so if he kills Duncan he's likely to end up being killed himself.
   - As Duncan's "kinsman" and "host" he has a duty to protect him.
   - Duncan is a good king — he's "clear in his great office", so killing him will lead to "deep damnation".
   - Macbeth knows his own ambition will be his downfall.
2) Lady Macbeth is forceful — she bullies and persuades Macbeth to go through with the murder by questioning his masculinity. She says that by killing Duncan Macbeth will be "so much more the man". This has a double meaning — he'll be more of a man, and he'll also be King.
3) She rejects her femininity by telling Macbeth that she'd kill her own child. She's trying to prove how remorseless and evil she is.

Writer's Techniques — Suspense

Act One ends with anticipation — the murder has been planned but hasn't happened. This builds suspense for the audience.

Writer's Techniques — Imagery

Lady Macbeth uses language connected with alchemy (the process of turning cheap metal into gold): "A limbeck" and "receipt" are the apparatus used and "fume" refers to the gases produced. Alchemists never succeeded in turning cheap metal into real gold — Shakespeare is hinting that Macbeth will never become a good king.

Lady Macbeth — putting the 'kill' in 'kilt'

So Duncan's all tucked up in bed, happy as Larry and chuffed that his thanes are so loyal and awesome. Little does he know what 'Mum of the Year' Lady Macbeth has in store for him. Someone really ought to tell him to loch oot...

Analysis of Act Two — Macbeth Murders Duncan

Macbeth kills Duncan, and Lady Macbeth covers the servants in blood to frame them for his murder.

*Scene 1 — The **Famous** 'dagger' bit*

1) Banquo and his son, Fleance, go for a walk at night. Fleance is a reminder to the audience about the Witches' prophecy that Banquo's sons will be kings.
2) There aren't any stars: "Their candles are all out", so it's very dark. The darkness symbolises the evil that Macbeth is about to do. The starless sky also echoes Duncan's speech in Act 1, Scene 4 about stars shining on the deserving — Macbeth is undeserving.

Character — Banquo

Banquo's response shows that he's more moral than Macbeth, but his "cursèd thoughts" and mention of the Witches may hint that he's thinking about acting on the prophecies.

© COLUMBIA / THE KOBAL COLLECTION

3) Macbeth promises that if Banquo supports him, he'll "honour" him, but Banquo replies that he'll only help Macbeth if he can keep his "allegiance clear". This shows that he's loyal to Duncan.

Theme — The Supernatural

See p.42 for more on visions.

In his soliloquy Macbeth talks about "witchcraft", "Hecate's offerings" and "a ghost". This links Macbeth to the Witches and shows how he's affected by their predictions. He starts seeing visions of a dagger — it's not clear if it's leading him to commit murder or warning him against it.

*Scene 2 — The deed is **Done***

Turning point in the action
Macbeth commits his first murder.

1) Lady Macbeth waits for Macbeth to return from killing Duncan. She's startled by every noise, and she says that she couldn't kill Duncan because he reminded her of her father. This suggests that Lady Macbeth isn't as merciless as she appears.
2) The murder takes place offstage — this increases the suspense and makes the audience imagine the killing, which makes it more horrific. It also lets the audience see how Macbeth and Lady Macbeth are affected by their experience in Duncan's room.
3) There's a lot of foreshadowing (hinting at things that happen later) in this scene:

- Macbeth doubts "Neptune's ocean" will clean the blood off his hands — he's feeling guilty. Lady Macbeth doesn't seem as bothered by her bloody hands — it's an ironic foreshadowing of her frenzied hand washing in Act 5.
- Macbeth says he's "murdered sleep" — sleep symbolises peace and a clear conscience, so murdering sleep shows that he's wracked with guilt. This also foreshadows Lady Macbeth's sleepwalking in Act 5.
- There are also references to insanity — Lady Macbeth talks about Macbeth going "mad" and being "brain-sickly" — it's an ironic foreshadowing of her own madness later.

For more on the symbolism of blood and water see p.57.

4) The stage directions add to the tension — there's a repetition of a knocking sound, which gives a sense of urgency. This seems to echo Macbeth's pounding heart, and is a sign of his fear and guilt.

Macbeth tried hard — he gave it a good stab...

Lady Macbeth says she can't kill Duncan 'cos he looked too much like her dad — wonder if that excuse works elsewhere? "Sorry, I can't eat this broccoli — the stalk reminds me of Great Uncle Percy." Pretty believable, eh?

Analysis of Act Two — The Body is Discovered

There's a bit of light relief (don't get used to it) in Scene 3 before Duncan's body is discovered.

*Scene 3 — Duncan's body is **Discovered***

1) The Porter's comic monologue relieves the tension, but also builds suspense before Duncan's body is found.
2) Shakespeare uses dramatic irony to increase the audience's anticipation — the audience knows that Duncan has been murdered, and although the characters don't know, they can sense evil:
   - The Porter describes the Macbeths' castle gate as a "hell-gate" and makes a joke about a man sent to hell who "committed treason".
   - Lennox comments on how "unruly" and stormy the night was — he tells Macbeth that the wind sounded like "strange screams of death".
   - He also says the storm was "prophesying with accents terrible / Of dire combustion and confused events". This reflects the terrible events that have taken place and foreshadows the events to come.

Treason means betraying your king or country.

3) Macduff finds Duncan's body — his reaction shows how horrified he is, and makes the murder seem even worse.
4) Macbeth confesses to killing Duncan's servants out of rage. When Lady Macbeth hears this she faints. This could be to distract the other characters from Macbeth's suspicious behaviour, or she may actually be horrified by Macbeth's violence, which she didn't help plan.

Writer's Techniques — Language

- Before Duncan's body is found, Macbeth speaks in short sentences — "'Twas a rough night", "Not yet" — he seems distracted and tense. This highlights his guilt and nervousness.
- When Duncan's body is discovered, Macbeth's language changes — he describes Duncan's "silver skin laced with his golden blood". His poetic language seems false.

5) Malcolm and Donalbain run away because they fear for their lives. It makes them look guilty and allows Macbeth to take the throne.

See p.40 for more about how Macbeth becomes King.

*Scene 4 — Macbeth is about to be made **King***

1) This scene is a bridge between Act 2 and Act 3. Its purpose is to create a sense of fear and uncertainty.
2) Strange events have happened since Duncan's death, which show how the natural order has been disrupted. A country's well-being is linked to that of its king, so these events are bad omens for Macbeth's reign.
   - It's dark during the day: "dark night strangles the travelling lamp". This symbolises the evil that has come over Scotland.
   - A falcon has been savagely killed by an owl — the falcon symbolises Duncan, and the owl symbolises Macbeth (see p.56).
   - Horses have been eating each other, which is unnatural.
3) The scene ends with Macduff telling Rosse that Macbeth will be King. Macduff isn't going to the coronation — this suggests he's suspicious of Macbeth and sets him up as Macbeth's main enemy.

Macbeth's speeches go on and on — at least Duncan got to the point...

The porter seems pretty perceptive — he makes a lot of ironic references to Macbeth's dirty deed and thinks the castle is like the gate of hell. Then he goes and ruins his credibility by chatting about sex and having a chunder. Nice.

Analysis of Act Three — Macbeth Plots Banquo's Murder

That naughty Macbeth is up to no good again — this time he's got his sights set on Banquo...

*Scene 1 — Macbeth plots Banquo's **Murder***

© Amitava Sarkar

1) The scene opens with Banquo's soliloquy.
   His inner thoughts reveal several things:
   - He's suspicious of Macbeth, who he thinks "play'dst most foully" for the crown.
   - He's still thinking about the Witches' prediction that his descendants will be kings. He's ambitious, but unlike Macbeth, he's willing to let fate take its course.
2) Macbeth's soliloquy shows that his attitude to murder has changed. In Act 1 he was tormented by killing Duncan and almost couldn't do it, but he's decisive about killing Banquo — murder has become easy.
3) Macbeth hires murderers to kill Banquo. This shows how much his character has changed — in Act 1, Scene 1 he was a fearless hero, but now he can't meet his enemy face-to-face. He's become a coward.
4) Macbeth has become more like Lady Macbeth. He persuades the murderers to do what he wants by questioning their masculinity and telling lies to convince them that Banquo is their enemy.

Theme — Fate and Free Will

Macbeth thinks he can change fate and prevent Banquo's descendants from becoming kings by killing Banquo and Fleance.

*Scene 2 — The Macbeths are feeling **Insecure***

1) Lady Macbeth and Macbeth both feel insecure about Macbeth's position as King.
2) Shakespeare uses oxymorons in this scene, e.g. "doubtful joy" and "restless ecstasy", to show their mixed emotions. They've got what they wanted but they also feel guilty and uneasy.

An oxymoron is where two words contradict each other.

Character — The Macbeths

There's evidence that Macbeth and Lady Macbeth have switched roles — before she told him to "look like / th' innocent flower" — now he tells her to flatter Banquo and says that they must make their "faces vizards to our hearts".

3) This scene shows a change in the Macbeths' relationship. Macbeth hints that he plans to kill Banquo, but he refuses to confide in Lady Macbeth. This could be because he wants to protect Lady Macbeth from more guilt, or because he's so driven by his own ambition that her opinion doesn't matter.
4) Macbeth uses a lot of animal imagery in this scene, e.g. "full of scorpions is my mind" and "the bat has flown". This sets an unsettling tone — these animals remind the audience of evil and emphasise Macbeth's feelings of insecurity and paranoia.

Writer's Techniques — Foreshadowing

Macbeth envies Duncan because he isn't troubled by "Malice domestic, foreign levy" (civil war or foreign armies). This foreshadows Macduff's uprising and the English attack at the end of the play.

Maybe Macbeth won't kill him — but I wouldn't Banquo'n it...

Macbeth has definitely got some sort of inferiority complex going on — maybe Duncan didn't ask him to play football with the other thanes? Or Banquo didn't invite him to his birthday feast? Or maybe he's just one crazy son-of-a-gun.

Analysis of Act Three — Banquo is Murdered

Banquo bites the dust, Fleance escapes and Banquo's ghost makes an unwelcome appearance at the feast.

Scene 3 — Banquo is ***Murdered***

© Everett Collection / Rex Features

1) A third murderer joins the other murderers as they prepare to kill Banquo. Macbeth has sent another murderer because he's paranoid and doesn't trust anyone. Some directors emphasise this by making Macbeth the third murderer.
2) The sun is setting and darkness is coming — this symbolises the terror of Macbeth's reign. Banquo approaches carrying a torch — the light symbolises Banquo's goodness. When he's murdered the light goes out — his goodness has been destroyed.
3) Fleance escapes — the Witches' prediction about Banquo's sons becoming kings could still come true. This shows that it's impossible to cheat fate, which suggests that Macbeth would have become King even if he hadn't forced it to happen.

Scene 4 — Macbeth sees Banquo's ***Ghost***

Turning point in the action
The Thanes start to question Macbeth's sanity.

1) The Macbeths hold a feast. Macbeth's in a good mood because he thinks that Banquo and Fleance are being dealt with. He's happy to "play the humble host" — the word "play" suggests his hospitality is fake.
2) One of the murderers tells Macbeth that he's killed Banquo but Fleance has escaped. Macbeth replies that he's "cabined, cribbed, confined". The alliteration emphasises how trapped he feels. With Fleance still alive Macbeth knows that his future as King is uncertain.
3) Banquo's ghost appears after Macbeth receives the news about Banquo's death and Fleance's escape — it's a symptom of his guilt and anxiety. The ghost is an important dramatic device:

Theme — The Supernatural
In the previous scene Macbeth envied Duncan because he was at peace, but the ghost of Banquo suggests to Macbeth that even in death he won't be able to rest.

- Only Macbeth can see the ghost, so the audience is unsure whether it's real or a trick of Macbeth's guilty conscience. The ghost appears when Macbeth says Banquo's name — this suggests that it is a guilt-inspired hallucination. It echoes the ghostly dagger that Macbeth saw before Duncan's murder.
- The ghost sits on Macbeth's throne — this is a visual and dramatic reminder to the audience of the Witches' prophecy that Banquo's descendants will be kings.

4) Macbeth's behaviour is so strange that Lady Macbeth has to pretend that he's unwell. She takes control again, and echoes Act 1, Scene 7 when she asks him, "Are you a man?" She thinks his fear isn't manly.
5) Macbeth says, "It will have blood they say — blood will have blood." His repetition of the word "blood" shows his fear — he's starting to see the inevitability of his downfall.

Character — Macbeth
Macbeth says he's killed so many people that "Returning were as tedious as go o'er". He's despairing here — he doesn't want to keep killing, but he thinks it's the only way to secure the throne.

Poor Banquo — he didn't have a ghost of a chance...

Some productions choose to have the actor who plays Banquo come on stage as the ghost, but some directors don't cast anyone as the ghost so Macbeth looks like he's shouting at nothing — this makes Macbeth look extra-crazy.

Analysis of Act Three — The Thanes are Unhappy

Hecate makes a cameo appearance and the lords are getting antsy...

Scene 5 — The Witches meet with **Hecate**

© Amitava Sarkar

1) The Goddess of Witches, Hecate, is annoyed that the three Witches have been meddling in Macbeth's business without involving her.

Writer's Techniques — Mood and Atmosphere

This is a dark scene which creates an atmosphere of fear and evil.

Theme — Fate and Free Will

Hecate says that Macbeth "shall spurn fate" — he thinks that he can change the course of destiny and stop Banquo's descendants from being King.

2) The Witches plan to summon apparitions to trick Macbeth into being overconfident: "security / Is mortals' chiefest enemy." By making him bold they're making sure he'll continue his reign of terror — plunging natural order into chaos.

Scene 6 — Lennox plans an **Uprising**

1) This is another bridge scene, between Act 3 and Act 4. The minor characters tell the audience everything that's happened — Macduff has raised an army against Macbeth, while Malcolm is at the English court.

2) Lennox suspects that Macbeth's responsible for Duncan and Banquo's murders. He's careful not to speak his mind about Macbeth because he knows Macduff "lives in disgrace" for not being loyal to the King. However, Lennox's true feelings are revealed by his speech:

- The tone of his monologue is sarcastic, e.g. he says Duncan's murder "did grieve Macbeth!" — he means the exact opposite.
- He uses rhetorical questions: "To kill their gracious father?" — he doesnt believe that Malcolm and Donalbain murdered Duncan.
- His speech is full of exclamations such as "But, peace!" and "Damnèd fact!" This shows how angry he is, but also hints that he's afraid to show his anger — his short, broken sentences suggest he's trying to hold back his emotions.

Historical Context

In Shakespeare's time, people thought that the King was appointed by God, so when the Lord calls King Edward "holy", this shows he's the rightful King of England. The Lord says that Malcolm will have help from "Him above" — they believe he's the rightful King of Scotland, so God will help him overcome Macbeth.

Writer's Techniques

Shakespeare wrote this scene from the perspective of the minor characters to develop the feeling of unrest in Scotland.

3) Lennox ends the scene by sending a message to the English court to free them from the "hand accursed" — this builds the tension because it becomes a question of how far Macbeth will go before he's stopped. The audience sees that Macbeth's death is inevitable, and the only way to restore peace to Scotland.

You've got to Fife for your rights...

The lords are pretty annoyed that Scotland has gone to the dogs — there's not enough food, everyone's paranoid that Macbeth will be after them next, and they've had enough of bodies turning up after feasts. Tough break, lads.

Analysis of Act Four — Macbeth Visits the Witches

The Witches are back by popular demand — have your beard trimmers at the ready...

Scene 1 — The *Witches* make more *Predictions*...

© Amitava Sarkar

1) The scene opens with the Witches casting a spell — "Double, double toil and trouble". This reminds the audience of their evil intentions, and the word "double" hints at double meanings.
2) The gruesome list of body parts that the Witches throw into the cauldron sets a dark, frightening tone.
3) They announce Macbeth's arrival by saying, "Something wicked this way comes" — this shows how much he's changed from the brave hero of Act One.
4) The Witches pretend to obey him: "Speak. / Demand. / We'll answer." They trick him into asking for the apparitions by saying that he can talk to their "masters" — the Witches know Macbeth's biggest weakness is his ambition, so they play on his lust for power.

Writer's Techniques

Macbeth says, "though the yeasty waves / Confound and swallow navigation up", which extends the metaphor that Macbeth is a sailor and Scotland is a ship (see p.10).

Turning point in the action
The Witches make Macbeth believe he's invincible.

...and *Summon Apparitions* to predict the *Future*

1) Macbeth's language is confident at the start of the scene. He uses commands such as "Tell me" and "Call 'em" to control the Witches and threatens them with "an eternal curse" — he's not afraid of them.
2) The Witches summon three apparitions to predict his future — they symbolise the threats to Macbeth:

Apparition	Interpretation
An armoured head warns Macbeth about Macduff.	• The armoured head could foreshadow Macbeth's decapitation. • It could also symbolise treachery and the violence of battle.
A bloody child tells Macbeth that no one born from a woman can harm him.	• This could represent Macduff, born by Caesarean section.
A child wearing a crown and carrying a branch tells Macbeth that he can't be beaten until Birnam Wood moves to Dunsinane Hill.	• This could represent Malcolm — the rightful heir. • The wood could represent Birnam Wood, but also the hope that Scotland might grow and flourish under Malcolm's rule.

The stage directions say that each apparition "Descends" — this suggests that they're going back to hell.

3) Macbeth takes the Witches' predictions at face value, even though he knows that people who trust the Witches are "damned". He's desperate for them to give him good news to make him feel secure.

By the pricking of my thumbs, the end of the section this way comes...

This scene has the potential to be terrifying when it's performed — severed heads and bloody children whizzing about the stage. Although low-budget productions may just have a plastic doll smeared in ketchup dangled about on a string.

Analysis of Act Four — Lady Macduff is Murdered

Macbeth's on a killing spree — next on the list is Lady Macduff and son...

...*Macbeth's* full of *Confidence*

1) The apparitions give Macbeth confidence. He thinks that he'll never be defeated because it's impossible for Birnam Wood to move and that he's invincible because every man is born from a woman.
2) He wants to know if the Witches' prophecy about Banquo is true, so they show him another vision — a line of Banquo's descendants. Macbeth is angry: "Thy crown does sear mine eyeballs."

Theme — Reality and Appearances

Although the Witches haven't lied, they've deliberately misled Macbeth. It's another example of their deception.

Historical Context

Some of Banquo's descendants carry orbs and sceptres to show that they will be rulers of England as well as Scotland. *Macbeth* was written during the reign of King James, who ruled over Scotland and England.

3) Macbeth wants to kill Macduff's family — this shows how evil and paranoid he's become. He's willing to kill anyone associated with his enemy even if they don't pose a threat.
4) He doesn't discuss the murders with Lady Macbeth any more — he's driven solely by his own ambition and trusts no one.

Scene 2 — Macbeth has Lady Macduff and her son Murdered

1) Lady Macduff is angry and scared because her husband has run off and left her to protect their castle and children.
2) Her fear shows how afraid people are under Macbeth's rule. Her comment, "to do harm / Is often laudable", shows how the morals of Scotland have been turned upside down by Macbeth's tyranny.
3) Lady Macduff talks with her son — their witty dialogue shows their maternal bond. The caring character of Lady Macduff contrasts with Lady Macbeth, who would have "dashed the brains out" of her own child.
4) The murderer enters and stabs Lady Macduff's son — it's made even more brutal by the murderer calling him "egg" and "fry", which highlights how young he is and shows that Macbeth is willing to kill defenceless children. It also shows that he's too cowardly to commit the murders himself.
5) The murder of Lady Macduff's son happens on stage — this symbolises the fact that Macbeth no longer cares if people see his terrible crimes.

Writer's Techniques — Language

Shakespeare starts this scene mid-dialogue. This highlights the confusion that Lady Macduff feels about her husband leaving.

© Amitava Sarkar

Writer's Techniques — Symbolism

Lady Macduff compares herself to a wren, a tiny, powerless bird, protecting her nest from an owl (Macbeth). This reminds the audience of the imagery of the owl killing the falcon in Act 2, Scene 4 and shows that Macbeth is now killing defenceless 'prey'.

Lady Macduff kicks the bucket — Och Aye, the Noooooooooooooo....

Poor Lady Macduff and her young son never stood a chance — they were sitting ducks. But on the bright side, Macbeth's definitely doing his bit for the Scottish economy — I bet business is booming at the funeral parlour...

Analysis of Act Four — Malcolm and Macduff Meet

There's a lot of talking in this scene — it might seem a bit dull, but it's important stuff.

*Scene 3 — Malcolm **Tests** Macduff's **Loyalty***

1) Macduff goes to England to convince Malcolm to raise an army against Macbeth. Malcolm doesn't trust Macduff — this shows the fear and suspicion Macbeth's created.

Theme — Loyalty

Macduff shows his loyalty to Scotland by going to England to support Malcolm even though his family is in danger.

Theme — Kingship

- Malcolm has learnt from Duncan's mistakes — he doesn't blindly trust the thanes. This caution suggests that he'll be a better king than Duncan.
- Malcolm tells Macduff that he's honest, grateful and god-fearing — good qualities for a king. Malcolm's loyalty to his country contrasts with Macbeth's tyranny and betrayal.

2) Malcolm thinks that because Macduff's family hasn't been harmed he must support Macbeth. This creates dramatic irony — the audience knows that Macduff's family has been murdered.
3) Malcolm tests Macduff's loyalty by pretending to be more evil than Macbeth. Macduff passes Malcolm's test by proving that he's loyal to Scotland and won't support another tyrant.
4) Shakespeare contrasts the kind, unselfish kingship of Edward with the cruel, selfish tyranny of Macbeth.

Theme — Supernatural

Edward has "a heavenly gift of prophecy" and can cure the sick with his touch. Since rightful kings were thought to have been appointed by God, people thought that Edward had divine gifts — the opposite of the Witches' evil, supernatural powers.

Like Macbeth, Malcolm tries to disguise his true nature — but he does it to protect Scotland, rather than for his own gain.

*... and **Macduff** discovers that his **Family** has been **Murdered***

1) Rosse arrives and tells Macduff that his family have been killed — his reluctance to break the news creates drama.
2) Macduff's grief is clear from the way he speaks: "All my pretty ones? / Did you say all? O hell-kite! All? / What, all my pretty chickens" His short sentences, rhetorical questions and repetition of the word "all" shows that he can't believe what Rosse has told him.
3) The murder of Macduff's family is important to the plot — it motivates Macduff to get revenge on Macbeth and end his cruel reign.

Writer's Techniques — Symbolism

See p.57 for more on masculinity.

Like the Macbeths, Malcolm thinks masculinity means being aggressive — he tells Macduff to "Dispute it like a man". Macduff contrasts this by saying he should "feel it as a man" — he believes that men are also sensitive. In this way, Macduff teaches Malcolm how to be a good man and king.

King Edward — the original Mr Potato Head...

Macbeth was written and performed during the reign of King James I, who was thought to be a descendant of the real Banquo. Shakespeare lays the flattery on thick — divine rights this, compassionate monarch that — what a suck-up.

Analysis of Act Five — Lady Macbeth Sleepwalks

Lady Macbeth has gone a bit cuckoo and gives the game away. Meanwhile, the nobles prepare for war.

*Scene 1 — Lady Macbeth has gone **Mad***

© Amitava Sarkar

1) It's the first time the audience sees Lady Macbeth since things have started to go wrong — her character has completely changed. She's been driven mad by guilt and fear:

- She carries a candle and "has light by her continually" — she's afraid of the dark. It's ironic because in Act 1, Scene 5 she welcomes the darkness: "Come, thick night". Night now reminds her of the evil she's done.
- She tries to wash imaginary blood off her hands: "Out, damned spot!" Hand-washing symbolises her guilt, and contrasts with her attitude in Act 2, Scene 2 when she tells Macbeth "A little water clears us of this deed."

See pages 55-57 for more on imagery.

2) The way her language changes also reveals her guilty conscience:

- Her speech changes from smooth and fluent blank verse to disjointed prose — this shows her troubled state of mind.
- Her speech is uncertain: "The Thane of Fife had a wife — where is she now?" Her use of questions shows her mental confusion and contrasts with her domineering language in Act 1, Scene 7.

Shakespeare uses Lady Macbeth's sleepwalking to reveal her inner thoughts.

3) The Doctor says "unnatural deeds / Do breed unnatural troubles" — Lady Macbeth has upset the natural balance by doing evil things. It reminds the audience of the unnatural things reported in Act 2, Scene 4.

*Scene 2 — The Thanes prepare for **Battle***

1) The Scottish lords are preparing to attack Macbeth. This scene builds tension in anticipation of the battle.
2) They plan to meet the English army near Birnam Wood — it's a reminder of the Witches' prophecy, and hints that Macbeth might be defeated.
3) Shakespeare uses imagery to extend metaphors which have been running throughout the play:

- Health — the lords use imagery to describe Scotland as unwell. Caithness talks about "the sickly weal" (wound) and refers to Malcolm as the "med'cine" that will heal the country.
- Nature — Lennox describes Malcolm as the "sovereign flower". He also wants to "drown the weeds" (get rid of Macbeth). He compares Macbeth to a weed because he's preventing anything else from growing and he's destroying the land.
- Clothing — Angus describes Macbeth as a "dwarfish thief" wearing a "giant's robe" — the responsibility of being King is too great for Macbeth.

For more on imagery have a look at pages 55-57.

Writer's Techniques — Imagery

Angus describes Macbeth's "murders sticking on his hands" — this reminds the audience of Lady Macbeth trying to wash the blood from her hands.

Macbeth walks into a bar...

... he orders a Bloody Mary for Lady Macbeth and a whisky for himself. The barman asks, "What about your friend in the corner?" Macbeth replies, "Oh, the Ghost of Banquo isn't fussy, but he likes his spirits." HAHAHAHA. Sigh.

Analysis of Act Five — Lady Macbeth Dies

These scenes alternate between Macbeth's castle and the armies on the battlefield — it's all getting pretty tense...

*Scenes 3 and 4 — Everyone **Prepares** for **Battle***

1) Like the rest of the scenes in Act 5, Scenes 3 and 4 are very short. Short scenes increase the pace and add to the drama.
2) Macbeth's soliloquy suggests he's beginning to despair even though he thinks he's invincible — "I have lived long enough". He admits that everything he's done is worthless.

Writer's Techniques

Macbeth's servant is called "Seyton", which sounds like Satan — this adds to the hellish image of Macbeth's castle.

© COLUMBIA / THE KOBAL COLLECTION

3) However, when he talks to other characters he's over-confident, giving orders like "Give me my armour", and calling his servant "lily-livered". This contrast reflects his unstable state of mind.
4) Macbeth shows signs of going mad — he tells Seyton to help him put his armour on and then almost straight away he says "Pull't off". He's confused and unbalanced. His mental state matches Lady Macbeth's — the Doctor says she's "troubled with thick coming fancies".
5) Meanwhile, Malcolm tells his soldiers to cut down branches from Birnam Wood to disguise their numbers — the audience sees that the Witches have tricked Macbeth, and that his defeat seems inevitable.
6) The English army calmly discuss their battle plan — they're in control. This contrasts with Macbeth's frenzied behaviour in Scene 3.

*Scene 5 — Lady Macbeth **Dies***

Lady Macbeth dies offstage — it's an anticlimax and shows how unimportant she's become.

1) Macbeth alternates between arrogance and despair in these scenes — this shows how confused he is.
2) At the start of the scene he's boasting and full of bravado. He says that he's "supped full with horrors", so nothing can frighten him. His attitude changes when he's told that his wife is dead:

- He realises that all his terrible acts had no purpose, "Signifying nothing".
- He describes life as a "shadow" and a "candle" — it's fleeting and unreal.
- He compares life to a "poor player" (actor) — he sees life as meaningless.
- His language, e.g. "petty", "fools" and "idiot", reflects his bitterness.

Writer's Techniques — Language

Macbeth's language is sad and reflective, e.g. he says "Life's but a walking shadow". This shows that he's not a monster — he still has a human side that regrets what he's done.

3) When Macbeth finds out that Birnam Wood is moving towards his castle, he realises that the Witches have tricked him: "the fiend / That lies like truth". This shows that he was too trusting of the Witches — it's ironic considering his betrayal of Duncan, who trusted Macbeth.
4) Macbeth decides to attack the approaching army — it's a brave decision and a reminder of the fearless warrior that Macbeth was in Act 1.

Turning point in the action
Macbeth starts to realise the Witches have tricked him.

When you're north of the border you never get away Scot-free...

Oh dear, oh dear. Things aren't looking rosy for Macbeth. His wife's had enough and topped herself, the armies are advancing and Birnam Wood seems to be moving towards the castle. Time to lock the doors and hide under the bed.

Analysis of Act Five — Macbeth is Killed

So here it is, the final page of analysis. Get through this and reward yourself with the questions over the page.

Scenes 6 and 7 — The Attack

1) Malcolm's army march towards Macbeth's castle and Macbeth's surrounded. Macbeth meets Young Siward and kills him — his death gives Macbeth confidence.
2) Macbeth is still clinging to the idea that he's invincible and chooses to trust the Witches' prophecies, even though the prediction about Birnam Wood has come true.

Writer's Techniques — Stagecraft

There are a lot of entrances and exits in Scene 7, which add to the confusion of the battle. They also add tension — Macduff is searching for Macbeth and enters the scene just after Macbeth exits.

Scene 8 — Macduff and Macbeth Fight

1) Macbeth and Macduff meet but Macbeth doesn't want to fight. He feels guilty about killing Macduff's family — "my soul is too much charged / With blood of thine already." He's still got some humanity left.
2) Macbeth still thinks he can't be harmed by any one "of woman born", but Macduff reveals that he was born by Caesarean section. Macbeth accepts that he's been misled by the Witches and says, "be these juggling fiends no more believed".
3) Macbeth is trapped but he refuses to back down, even though he knows he's doomed. This is a return to the brave warrior of Act 1, and shows that he's in his element fighting man to man rather than having people murdered.

Theme — Fate and Free Will

All the Witches' prophecies have come true. The prophecies are partly self-fulfilling, because Macbeth has brought about his own downfall through his actions.

The audience feels relief when Macbeth dies — this shows how evil he's become.

Scene 9 — Malcolm becomes King

1) Macbeth is dead and Malcolm has won. Malcolm is concerned about the missing members of his army — his caring nature contrasts with Macbeth's cruelty and ruthlessness.
2) Siward discovers that his son's been killed, but he's not upset. He thinks that it's an honour that his son died protecting Scotland. This shows how desperately they wanted to overthrow Macbeth.
3) Macduff enters with Macbeth's head. The play begins and ends with a battle and a traitor being beheaded — this gives the play a circular structure (see p.47).

Theme — Kingship

At the end of the play the natural order is restored. Malcolm is the rightful King and will be guided by God — he says, "by the grace of Grace, / We will perform in measure, time and place."

Writer's Techniques — Symbolism

Siward only cares that his son died bravely "like a man". Malcolm says that "He's worth more sorrow" — this shows that he's realised that being a man means more than just being violent and aggressive.

Calm down Macbeth — don't lose your head...

It all ends how it began — victory on the battlefield with a traitor's head being cut off. The circular structure ties everything up nicely. Either that or Shakespeare just ran out of ideas — but saying that won't impress the examiner.

Practice Questions

These questions will help you make sure you know exactly what happens when in *Macbeth* and what it all means. Your answers to the Quick Questions shouldn't be much longer than a sentence, but the answers to the In-depth Questions should be about a paragraph. Make sure you refuel with tea and biscuits before having a go at the Exam-style Questions on the next page.

Quick Questions

1) In Act One, what do the three Witches predict Macbeth will become?
2) What do the Witches predict will happen to Banquo's descendants?
3) What supernatural thing does Macbeth see in Act 2, Scene 1?
4) Why do Malcolm and Donalbain run away after Duncan's murdered?
5) Whose son escapes from the murderers in Act Three?
6) Pick one of the apparitions and describe briefly what it looks like and what it predicts.
7) Where has Malcolm run away to when Macduff finds him in Act Four?
8) What does Lady Macbeth try to wash off her hands in Act Five?
9) Who kills Macbeth?

In-depth Questions

1) In Act 1, Scene 3 Banquo says of the Witches' predictions:

   "The instruments of darkness tell us truths,
   Win us with honest trifles – to betray's" (124-125)

   Do you think Banquo is right? Use evidence from the play to support your answer.

2) "Macbeth never shows any remorse for what he has done."
   Do you agree with this statement? Explain your answer.

3) Do you think that Macbeth would have become King even if he hadn't killed anyone?
   Explain your answer.

Practice Questions

It's time for some hardcore questions to really test your noggin. Even if you don't have time to have a stab at all of them, try to write a plan for each question — it's all good practice. If you're revising for the Controlled Assessment task, remember that you might be asked to make links with another text.

Exam-style Questions

1 Answer **both** parts **(a)** and **(b)**.

a) What does the following extract contribute to the plot and themes of the play?

b) How does Shakespeare develop the plot and themes of this scene in another scene later in the play?

MACBETH (Aside) Two truths are told,
As happy prologues to the swelling act
Of the imperial theme. — I thank you, gentlemen. —
This supernatural soliciting 130
Cannot be ill, cannot be good. If ill,
Why hath it given me earnest of success,
Commencing in a truth? I am Thane of Cawdor.
If good, why do I yield to that suggestion,
Whose horrid image doth unfix my hair 135
And make my seated heart knock at my ribs
Against the use of nature? Present fears
Are less than horrible imaginings.
My thought, whose murder yet is but fantastical,
Shakes so my single state of man that function 140
Is smothered in surmise, and nothing is,
But what is not.

BANQUO Look how our partner's rapt.

MACBETH If chance will have me King, why, chance may crown me,
Without my stir.

BANQUO New honours come upon him
Like our strange garments, cleave not to their mould, 145
But with the aid of use.

(Act 1, Scene 3, 127-146)

Controlled Assessment-style Questions

1 How does Shakespeare use soliloquies in *Macbeth*?

2 How does the character of Macbeth change throughout the play?

3 Discuss the way Shakespeare presents the Witches in *Macbeth*.

Character Profile — Macbeth

Macbeth's the main character. Not surprising, really, given what the play's called. You'll have to write about him in any essay to do with this play — so you have to know what he's like.

*Macbeth is **Ambitious** but easily led **Astray***

1) Macbeth is a strong warrior who fights bravely in battle.
2) He's ambitious — he wants to become King of Scotland and will do anything to make this happen, even commit murder.
3) However, he's got a conscience and often doubts whether he's doing the right thing. He spends a lot of time feeling guilty.
4) He's easily influenced by others, which means he can be weak.

Language

The way Macbeth speaks reflects his state of mind. He asks lots of questions when he's feeling uncertain or guilty: "Whence is that knocking? / How is't with me, when every noise appals me?". At the start and end of the play, his language is more certain and confident: "Stars, hide your fires", "I will not yield".

Macbeth is...

ambitious: "I have no spur / To prick the sides of my intent, but only / Vaulting ambition"

brave: "brave Macbeth — well he deserves that name"

guilty: "Will all great Neptune's ocean wash this blood / Clean from my hand?

*He's a **Brave Hero**...*

1) At the start of the play, Macbeth is described as a "valiant" warrior. Rosse compares him to "Bellona's bridegroom" — he's saying that Macbeth is like Mars, the god of war.
2) Macbeth's brave actions impress the King, who names him Thane of Cawdor. This title shows that the King recognises Macbeth's "personal venture" (how bravely he fought) and loyalty.
3) Macbeth seems most comfortable on the battlefield. When he's fighting, he doesn't have to worry about his guilty conscience and the morality of his actions.
4) Macbeth dies in battle too — he fights "bear-like" to the end, even though he knows he's doomed. He's determined to "try the last" and says that he "will not yield".

Writer's Techniques — Structure

By the end of the play, Macbeth's come full circle — he's returned to being the brave soldier he was in Act 1. This contrasts with the middle of the play, where he seems weak and uncertain.

*...and a **Brutal Murderer***

1) Macbeth's brave but he's also a cold and calculating killer. He murders Duncan because he wants to be King. He also has Macduff's family and Banquo killed because he's worried about losing his position.
2) Macbeth is influenced by the people around him. He lets Lady Macbeth persuade him to kill Duncan because he wants to become King — his ambition is stronger than his morality.
3) At the end of the play, Macduff calls Macbeth a "hell-hound" and Young Siward calls him "abhorrèd tyrant" — Macbeth's violent ambition has ruined all his noble characteristics.

Theme — Fate and Free Will

When Macbeth says, "I am settled and bend up / Each corporal agent to this terrible feat", it sounds like he's making a deliberate decision to kill Duncan. Later, he says that he didn't have control over his actions because he's just a "poor player" who's controlled by fate (or he could be trying to make himself feel less guilty about his crimes).

Character Profile — Macbeth

He *Struggles* with his *Conscience*

1) Macbeth has a strong sense of right and wrong. He worries about the consequences of his actions because there's "judgement" on earth and "deep damnation" after death. This makes his actions more shocking.
2) He's reluctant to kill Duncan, who has "honoured" him, and says, "We will proceed no further in this business". He sounds confident, as if he's made up his mind — Macbeth recognises that Duncan trusts him as "his kinsman" and that as Duncan's "host" he has a duty to protect him.
3) Once he's killed Duncan, Macbeth swings between killing anyone who threatens his position as King and moments of despair when he struggles with terrible guilt.
4) His guilty conscience makes him imagine things:
   - Immediately after killing Duncan he hears a voice saying, "Macbeth does murder sleep".
   - After arranging for Banquo to be murdered, he sees Banquo's ghost at the feast and almost gives himself away. Lady Macbeth thinks he's hallucinating.
5) By the end of the play, Macbeth seems world-weary and cynical — he no longer seems to feel guilty, because he thinks that a person's actions don't matter and that life means "nothing".

Theme — Kingship

Macbeth knows that Duncan is a good king — "clear in his great office", and that killing him would damage Scotland. Macbeth places his own desires above his love of Scotland — this hints that he'll be a bad king.

He's easily *Influenced*

1) Lady Macbeth greatly influences Macbeth — he wouldn't kill Duncan if it wasn't for her. Macbeth acts because he doesn't want to be seen as unmanly or a "coward".
2) Lady Macbeth's influence over Macbeth declines after Duncan's murder — once he's murdered Duncan, the other murders seem to come more easily to Macbeth, so he acts alone.
3) He's also influenced by the supernatural:
   - The first time he meets the Witches, he trusts them straightaway, saying "Two truths are told". However, Banquo is suspicious of them and thinks they want to "win us to our harm".
   - He sees a dagger that leads him to Duncan's room.
   - As the Witches' prophecies start to come true, Macbeth's belief in them increases. He begins to rely more heavily on what they say, and panics when their prophecies are fulfilled unexpectedly.

Writer's Techniques — Symbolism

Lady Macbeth persuades Macbeth to kill Duncan by suggesting that he'll be "more the man". Throughout the play, Macbeth and Lady Macbeth link masculinity with strength and courage.

Macbeth is a Real Man...

Poor Macbeth — he wants to be good but he just can't stop murdering people. It's a shame because he starts off as such a nice guy (apart from the bit where he slices someone in half). It all goes downhill when his wife gets involved...

Character Profile — Lady Macbeth

It's difficult to say who would win in a fight between Lady Macbeth and a grizzly bear — but there's no doubt that she'd put up a good fight if she had to. She's tough as nails, this one...

Lady Macbeth's **Cruel** and **Ruthless**

1) Lady Macbeth is Macbeth's wife — she's an important character because she influences Macbeth, especially at the start of the play. She's ambitious and doesn't mind committing terrible crimes to get what she wants.
2) Lady Macbeth changes over the course of the play. At the beginning, she's dominant and confident — she persuades Macbeth that killing Duncan is the best thing to do.

Lady Macbeth is...

cruel: "And fill me from the crown to the toe topfull / Of direst cruelty"

cunning: "look like th'innocent flower, / But be the serpent under 't"

disturbed: "she is troubled with thick coming fancies"

© Amitava Sarkar

3) Once Macbeth has committed murder, Lady Macbeth is slowly driven mad by guilt. Macbeth distances himself from her and she kills herself because she can't live with what they've done.

She is very **Ambitious**

1) Lady Macbeth is just as ambitious as Macbeth — when she gets his letter, she immediately assumes that they need to kill Duncan. She's more ruthless than her husband.

Theme — Good and Evil

Lady Macbeth says that Macbeth is "too full o'th'milk of human kindness" — she thinks that his goodness makes him a "coward" and stops him from achieving his ambitions.

2) She knows that no ordinary woman would plan this murder. That's why she appeals to the spirit world to "unsex" her and fill her with "direst cruelty".

Writer's Techniques — Symbolism

Lady Macbeth links masculinity to strength and violence, but Shakespeare shows that women can be just as ruthless and cold-hearted as men.

3) Lady Macbeth knows her husband's weak spots — she uses his ambition and fear of being seen as a coward to manipulate him into killing Duncan.

She's **Clever** and **Quick-Witted**

1) Lady Macbeth is the one who comes up with the cunning plot to drug Duncan's servants and frame them for the murder. This shows that she's clever as well as cruel and heartless.

Theme — Reality and Appearances

If Lady Macbeth pretends to faint, she's taking advantage of the fact that she's a woman — she appears to be upset and emotional, when, in reality, she's cold-hearted and cruel.

2) When Duncan's murder is discovered, Lady Macbeth faints. This could be a pretence, which cleverly draws attention away from the unconvincing speech that Macbeth's making. Lady Macbeth also covers up Macbeth's strange behaviour when he thinks that he sees Banquo's ghost. She's the one in control of the situation.

Character Profile — Lady Macbeth

Shakespeare uses Lady Macbeth to **Explore Gender** and **Power**

1) Women are traditionally seen as kinder and weaker than men, but Shakespeare uses Lady Macbeth to show that this isn't always true. She says she would kill her own baby if she'd sworn to do it. Shakespeare contrasts her with Lady Macduff, who's a caring mother (see p.33).

2) Lady Macbeth does have a softer side. She says that she couldn't kill Duncan herself because he reminded her of her father. This shows that she's not as cold-hearted as she appears.

Writer's Techniques — Symbolism

Lady Macbeth thinks women are made weak by their maternal instincts — she tells the spirits to "Come to my woman's breasts / And take my milk for gall". She wants to lose her femininity.

Lady Macbeth's power lies in manipulating people. This shows that non-violent 'female' traits are just as powerful as violent 'male' ones.

Theme — Ambition

Macbeth is set in a violent, male-dominated society, so Lady Macbeth can only achieve her ambitions through Macbeth.

She Goes **Mad with Guilt** and **Kills Herself**

Language

The way Lady Macbeth speaks reflects her state of mind — at the beginning, she speaks confidently in verse. By the end, her speech is made up of mad ramblings and repetitions — "Come, come, come, come, give me your hand." It shows that she's lost all self-control.

1) At first, it's Macbeth who struggles with his guilty conscience. By the end of the play, Lady Macbeth is driven mad by guilt.

2) She starts sleepwalking. The doctor calls this a "great perturbation in nature" because her mind is so disturbed that it's affected her ability to sleep soundly.

3) In her sleep, she keeps washing her hands in the hope that she can wash away her feelings of guilt just as easily as the blood after Duncan's murder: "Out, damned spot!"

4) Guilt and isolation affect Lady Macbeth so much that she kills herself — she can't live with what she's done.

Writer's Techniques — Symbolism

Sleepwalking was thought to be unnatural in Shakespeare's time — sleep is the "Balm of hurt minds", so the fact that Lady Macbeth can't sleep peacefully emphasises her madness.

The Macbeths' **Marriage** is **Intense**

1) Macbeth and Lady Macbeth's relationship changes. At the beginning, their marriage seems loving and passionate — Macbeth calls Lady Macbeth "my dearest partner of greatness".

2) As the play develops, it becomes clear that Lady Macbeth dominates Macbeth — she manipulates him into killing Duncan and covers up his strange behaviour when he sees Banquo's ghost.

3) As Macbeth reveals less about his plans to his wife, Lady Macbeth becomes increasingly anxious and alone. Even though she's domineering at the beginning, she can't cope without her husband.

Lady Macbeth is always in the Macbath...

...though she'll never wash all that blood off her hands. Maybe if she was a bit more relaxed in the first place, she wouldn't have gone so loopy later in the play — all she needed was a night in with a bubble bath and a good book.

Character Profile — Duncan

Duncan's a nice guy, which is a shame because he's killed off by the end of Act 1. He influences a lot of the rest of the play though, so he's worth getting to know. It's a shame that nice guys always die first...

Duncan's **Kind**, but **Too Trusting**

1) Duncan's the King at the start of the play. He's a kind and generous man who rewards loyalty — he hands out honours to Macbeth and Malcolm.
2) Nobody has a bad word to say about Duncan — even Macbeth says that "his virtues / Will plead like angels".
3) Duncan's flaw is that he's too trusting. He trusts Macbeth and doesn't suspect he's plotting to kill him, and he describes the treacherous Thane of Cawdor as "a gentleman on whom I built / An absolute trust". However, Duncan can be firm when needed — he executes the Thane of Cawdor when he betrays him.

Duncan is...

kind: "let me enfold thee / And hold thee to my heart"

trusting: "There's no art / To find the mind's construction in the face"

a good king: "So clear in his great office"

He's an **Example** of a **Good King**

1) Shakespeare presents Duncan as a model king — he's kind, honest and fair.

Writer's Techniques — Symbolism

Duncan uses a lot of plant imagery — he says he will "plant" Macbeth and make sure he is "full of growing". This shows how he nurtures his subjects.

2) Macbeth says that one of the reasons that he shouldn't kill Duncan is because he's a good leader with many "virtues". Macduff also calls him "a most sainted king", reminding the audience that kings were thought to be chosen by God.
3) Duncan is kind, generous and trusting, and puts Scotland's needs ahead of his own. This contrasts with Macbeth, who is a bad king — he's a tyrant who's feared and hated. Macbeth puts his own selfish desires ahead of his country.

Theme — Kingship

In Act 4, Scene 3, Malcolm talks about what a good king should be like (see p.40). He says a ruler should have "stableness", "mercy" and "justice" — qualities that Duncan has.

Duncan **Isn't** like the **Other Men**

© Amitava Sarkar

1) Duncan isn't a soldier like Macbeth or Macduff — he's gentle and less aggressive. He doesn't fight himself, but sensibly sends his best soldiers to fight for him.
2) He's not afraid to be emotional — he shows "drops of sorrow" because he's so happy and talks about his "gentle senses" — this could be seen as unmanly.

Writer's Techniques — Symbolism

Duncan doesn't have the qualities that other characters associate with manliness, but Shakespeare shows that he's kind, fair and generous. This leads the audience to question whether a good leader really needs to be a violent warrior.

Duncan Donuts — where kings go when they're hungry...

The poor King didn't see it coming — as far as he knew, he was in for a night of feasting and merriment, not murder and betrayal. It goes to show that you should sleep with one eye open if you're round the Macbeths' house for dinner.

Character Profile — Malcolm and Donalbain

Malcolm and Donalbain are Duncan's sons. Malcolm is the eldest, and Duncan makes him his heir. This means that he should be the next King of Scotland, not Macbeth.

Malcolm and Donalbain **Learn** from their father's **Mistakes**

1) Malcolm is fair and honest, like his father. However, unlike Duncan, Malcolm and Donalbain are aware that they're in danger from those closest to them: "There's daggers in men's smiles, the near'r in blood, / The nearer bloody". They have the common sense to flee Scotland after Duncan is murdered.
2) Malcolm learns that he should only trust people who have proved their loyalty — when Macduff visits him, Malcolm tests his loyalty by pretending to be a tyrant. He knows that even people who seem good can be evil — "all things foul would wear the brows of grace".
3) In the end, Malcolm and Macduff make a good partnership because Macduff's experience gives Malcolm the confidence to take action.

Malcolm is...

wise: "wisdom plucks me / From over-credulous haste"

honest: "delight / No less in truth than life"

Malcolm and Donalbain aren't **Impulsive**

1) Malcolm and Donalbain don't react to their father's murder immediately. Malcolm says that their sorrow is too "strong" to act on it straight away. It shows that he's sensible and unwilling to act without waiting for the right time.
2) They're annoyed that Macbeth is making grand speeches which should be made by Duncan's sons — Malcolm asks Donalbain, "Why do we hold our tongues".

Theme — Reality and Appearance

Malcolm is more suspicious of false appearances than Duncan was — he says, "To show an unfelt sorrow is an office / Which the false man does easy." He's wary of people who seem fake, like Macbeth.

Malcolm **Develops** into a **Good Leader**

1) Malcolm becomes a confident leader. He earns the trust of the Scottish thanes, who say they will "give obedience where 'tis truly owed". They will follow Malcolm because he's the rightful King.
2) Malcolm eventually returns to Scotland with an army. He proves that he's clever by disguising the soldiers with branches, and leads his army to victory, which shows that he's a strong leader.
3) He rewards everyone who fought with him — like Duncan, he's generous to those who are loyal to him.

Theme — Kingship

Malcolm has many of the qualities that made Duncan a good King, but he's less naive than his father. This suggests that he'll eventually make a better King.

© Amitava Sarkar

Malcolm and his army, pretending to be trees, F.I.G.H.T.I.N.G...

It's amazing that Malcolm persuades a group of blood-hungry soldiers to dress up like a forest as part of his grand plan to get rid of Macbeth. They must have thought he'd gone mad... but it goes to show that the craziest ideas are the best.

Character Profile — Banquo

Banquo has a strange name but at least it doesn't begin with the letter 'M', like pretty much every other character. That's why I find the play so confusing — and why Banquo's secretly my favourite character.

Banquo** is more **Honourable** than **Macbeth

1) Banquo is a thane, like Macbeth. He's there when the Witches first make their prophecies.
2) Banquo is praised for his courage in battle — just like Macbeth. However, while Macbeth is guided by his own selfish desires, Banquo has "a wisdom that doth guide his valour". This suggests that Banquo thinks before he acts and does what is right.
3) Like Macbeth, Banquo is ambitious and hopes the Witches' prophecies come true. He doesn't act on their predictions, so he represents the path Macbeth could have chosen. Banquo isn't corrupted by his ambition like Macbeth is, so he remains honourable.
4) Macbeth promises to "honour" Banquo for his loyalty, but Banquo chooses to keep his "allegiance clear" — his conscience is more important to him than power and glory.

Banquo is...

brave: "that dauntless temper of his mind"

noble: "Noble Banquo, / That hast no less deserved"

wise: "The instruments of darkness tell us truths, / Win us with honest trifles – to betray's"

*Banquo **Doesn't Trust** the **Witches***

1) Banquo behaves rationally when he meets the Witches — he questions whether they are real, and doesn't trust them. In contrast, Macbeth wants them to tell him more, and is "rapt withal".

2) Banquo tells the Witches that he "neither beg nor fear / Your favours", but he's still intrigued to hear what they have to say. He admits to having "dreamt last night of the three weïrd sisters", which suggests he's still thinking about the predictions.

Theme — Reality and Appearance

Banquo's aware that the Witches could be "fantastical" and is perceptive enough to realise that they are "instruments of darkness" that could "win us to our harm". He's more cautious about believing what he sees than Macbeth is.

*He doesn't **Act** to **Protect Himself***

1) Banquo suspects that Macbeth murdered Duncan — "I fear, / Thou play'dst most foully". However, he doesn't act on his suspicions and instead reminds himself that he will be the "father / Of many kings" — this shows that ambitious thoughts can distract even the most honourable characters.
2) Macbeth sees Banquo as a threat — he says that there's no one except Banquo "Whose being I do fear". When Macbeth's hired killers surround him, Banquo's exclamation of "O, treachery!" shows that he didn't suspect that Macbeth would betray him.

Theme — Supernatural

Macbeth is haunted by Banquo's ghost, which shows how guilty Macbeth feels about killing his honourable friend.

Banquo wanted to Ban-quotes from all English essays...

...he didn't, in case you were wondering. In fact, if Banquo was a real person, he'd probably tell you to add some more snappy quotes to your Macbeth essays to show how well you know the play. He's so wise and trustworthy...

Character Profile — The Macduffs

The Macduffs make a good contrast with the Macbeths, and not just because their names look similar and both sound quite Scottish. Macduff's got more honour than Macbeth, but far fewer lines in the play...

*Macduff is **Honest** and **Sincere**...*

1) Macduff is a nobleman. He's honest and has integrity, so he acts as a contrast to Macbeth. He discovers Duncan's murder and is horrified by it.

Macduff is...

noble: "this noble passion, / Child of integrity"

a soldier: "I have no words: / My voice is in my sword"

emotional: "I must also feel it as a man"

2) Macduff doesn't go to Macbeth's coronation. This suggests that he is suspicious of Macbeth.

Writer's Techniques — Irony

Macduff is angry that, under Macbeth's rule, "New widows howl, new orphans cry". This is ironic, as his wife and children have just been murdered.

3) Macduff has a strong sense of loyalty and love for his country. He doesn't like the way Macbeth rules, so he goes to England to persuade Malcolm to help — he exclaims "O Scotland, Scotland!" which reflects his emotional turmoil about the state of his country.

4) Macduff is brave — he fights and kills Macbeth, freeing Scotland from "the tyrant".

*...but he puts his **Country** before his **Family***

1) Macduff makes a mistake by going to England, leaving his wife and children unprotected. His decision shows his strong sense of justice, but also his lack of "wisdom".

2) When he finds out that Macbeth has had them murdered, he is overcome with grief. His reaction shows his disbelief: "All my pretty ones? Did you say all?"

In contrast with the other men who see emotions as a sign of weakness, Macduff says that he will "feel" his grief "as a man". This shows that he sees the ability to show emotion as an important part of his masculinity.

3) Macduff kills Macbeth both to put the rightful heir on the throne and to avenge his family. He thinks that his wife and children will "haunt" him until he kills Macbeth.

*Lady Macduff can't **Understand** her husband's **Actions***

Theme — Good and Evil

Lady Macduff's goodness and caring behaviour towards her son contrast with Lady Macbeth's unnatural, evil desires — she says she'd kill her baby to get what she wants.

1) When Macduff goes to England, Lady Macduff says that he lacks "the natural touch" — she thinks his behaviour shows a lack of fatherly love.

2) Lady Macduff shows courage as she comforts her son, calling him "Poor bird". Her love and affection for him are clear. They speak in prose, which makes the scene feel natural and homely — this makes the murders even more shocking and horrible.

Macduff has it tough...

The scene where Macduff learns about his family's death is one of the saddest bits of the play — the page in my copy of *Macbeth* has gone all blurry with my tears. It's a shame that just one mistake costs Macduff his whole family...

Character Profile — The Witches

Some of the Witches' lines might sound a bit familiar, like "Double, double toil and trouble". They sound like something out of a weird creepy nursery rhyme and they lurk around the play like a bad smell...

*The **Witches** have **Supernatural Powers***

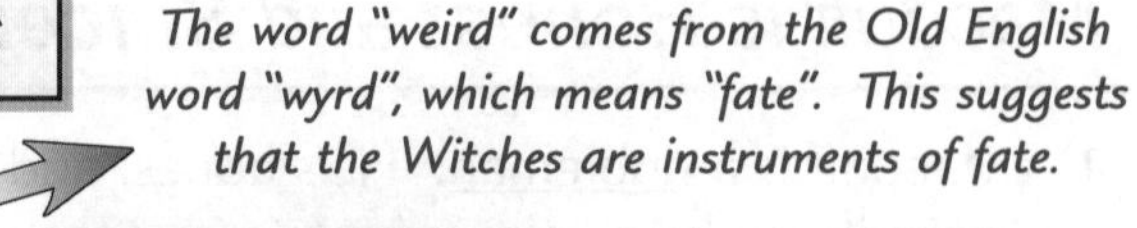

The word "weird" comes from the Old English word "wyrd", which means "fate". This suggests that the Witches are instruments of fate.

1) The Three Witches are also known as the Weïrd Sisters. They look like ugly women with beards, which suggests straight away that they're unnatural and evil.
2) The Witches can see the future — all their predictions come true eventually. They seem to act out of malice — they don't gain anything from their actions, they just like causing trouble.

The Witches are...

evil: "instruments of darkness"

ambiguous: "This supernatural soliciting / Cannot be ill, cannot be good."

strange: "So withered and so wild"

© Ellie Kurtz

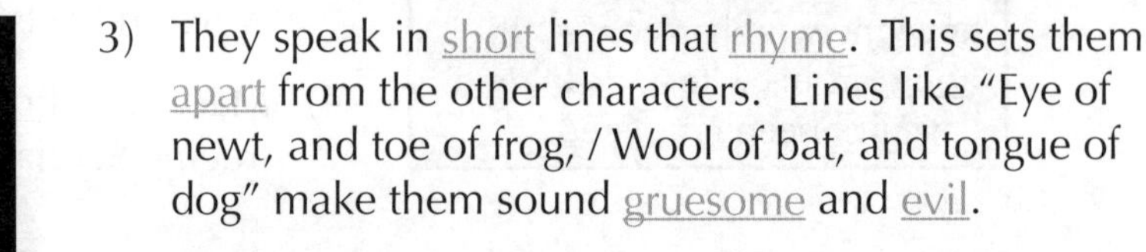

3) They speak in short lines that rhyme. This sets them apart from the other characters. Lines like "Eye of newt, and toe of frog, / Wool of bat, and tongue of dog" make them sound gruesome and evil.
4) Banquo isn't sure whether the Witches are real or imaginary — "Are ye fantastical, or that indeed / Which outwardly ye show?" He's suspicious that their appearance is misleading.

Theme — Reality and Appearance

The Witches' line "Fair is foul, and foul is fair" shows that nothing is as it seems in the play.

*They're **Evil**, but they **Don't** tell Macbeth to **Murder** Duncan*

1) The Witches are usually accompanied by "Thunder and lightning". This makes the atmosphere dark and frightening.
2) They make prophecies but they never explain how they'll happen. In this way, they take advantage of Macbeth's weakness (his "Vaulting ambition") and use it to control his actions.
3) The Witches don't tell Macbeth to murder Duncan — but they do predict he'll be king, which pushes him to kill Duncan.

Theme — Fate and Free Will

Shakespeare doesn't make it clear whether the Witches are messengers of fate (so their prophecies are inevitable) or whether Macbeth could change his future (see p.44).

This is a self-fulfilling prophecy — Macbeth makes it come true.

4) The Witches confuse Macbeth using paradoxes — for example, telling him that Banquo will be "Lesser than Macbeth, and greater". By not being clear about what the future holds, they keep control of Macbeth.
5) Hecate is the goddess of witchcraft. She's angry at Macbeth's behaviour, so she uses the apparitions to punish him. They trick him by making predictions that give him a false sense of security, such as "none of woman born / Shall harm Macbeth". These predictions indirectly lead to his death.

Eye of newt, and toe of examiner...

The Witches don't appear in that many scenes, but their predictions spark off the action of the play and influence Macbeth's actions. They might look and sound a bit odd but there's no doubt that they're up to no good...

Character Profile — Other Characters

Now you know who everyone important is. The other characters in the play are minor.
But you'd better know who they are, just so you don't get confused.

*There are some other **Noblemen**...*

© COLUMBIA / THE KOBAL COLLECTION

1) Lennox, Rosse, Menteith, Angus and Caithness are all thanes — Scottish noblemen. None of them are very significant characters. They're basically there to move the story along and show how power shifts during the play.
2) They comment on the big events of the play — e.g. in Act 3, Scene 6, Lennox sarcastically says that Macbeth "nobly" and "wisely" killed Duncan's guards. This shows that the thanes suspect that Macbeth killed Duncan, and suggests that he's starting to lose power.
3) The thanes say that they will "give obedience where 'tis truly owed" — in other words, they'll be loyal to whoever deserves it. They gradually start to question whether Macbeth is the rightful King, and start to resent his tyranny. By the end of the play they side with Malcolm and help him defeat Macbeth.

Rosse represents the noblemen who comment on the action but are reluctant to put themselves in danger. He warns Lady Macduff that "cruel are the times" but makes an excuse to leave before the murderers arrive. This leaves Lady Macduff, who he calls his "dearest coz", unprotected.

*...and a few **Other Minor Characters***

1) The Porter appears in Act 2. He's a comic character — he talks about his drunken behaviour the night before, saying that drinking makes three things happen, "nose-painting, sleep, and urine". He provides a bit of light relief in between the darker, more tragic parts of the plot.

Cultural Context

In Shakespeare's time, most plays had a clown-like character to amuse the crowd. Usually the clown would be in one or two scenes and would make some rude jokes or silly comments.

2) Three Murderers appear in Act 3 — they're hired killers that Macbeth persuades to kill Banquo and his son, Fleance. They kill Banquo but let Fleance escape. The Murderers show how ruthless Macbeth has become, and possibly that he's unwilling to commit more murders himself. They also kill Lady Macduff and her children on Macbeth's orders — this shows how desperate and cruel he is.

Macbeth sends a third murderer to help the first two kill Banquo — this shows that he no longer trusts anyone. Some people think the third murderer is Macbeth himself.

3) Siward is an English Lord. He's a great fighter and helps Malcolm defeat Macbeth in Act 5. He's got a son, Young Siward, who is killed in battle by Macbeth.

Theme — Loyalty and Betrayal

Siward shows how important honour and bravery are to him by saying he's glad that his son died an honourable death and showed loyalty to Malcolm.

4) There are a few other minor characters such as the Doctor and the Gentlewoman who are with Lady Macbeth when she goes mad. They only have small parts but they help to move the plot along and develop the themes of the play.

The Old Man and the Porter don't even have names...

...which is quite good really because there are lots of names to remember. These characters are quite minor but they do comment on the action and themes of the play — and slipping them into your essays will impress the examiner.

Practice Questions

These questions will help you make sure you know exactly who all the characters are and what they're like. There are a few characters with similar-sounding names in the play, so learn who's who and what each character does. It's also useful to learn who's alive and who's dead at the end of the play, so you don't make any embarrassing comments about a character who dies in Act 1.

Quick Questions

1) What title does Duncan give Macbeth in Act 1?

2) Give two reasons why Macbeth is reluctant to murder Duncan.

3) Which three words best describe Lady Macbeth:
a) caring b) cruel c) ambitious d) sweet e) mad?

4) Why does Lady Macbeth say that she couldn't murder Duncan?

5) Who are Malcolm and Donalbain?

6) Whose idea is it to disguise the army as a forest?

7) What does Banquo suspect Macbeth did in order to become King?

8) Why does Macduff leave his family to go to England?

9) Find three quotes from the play that describe the Three Witches.

In-depth Questions

1) Do you think Macbeth is a brave soldier, a cold-hearted killer or both?
Find evidence from the play to back up your answer.

2) Explain how Shakespeare shows that Lady Macbeth has a guilty conscience.
How does this affect your feelings about her?

3) Compare Banquo and Macbeth's reactions to the Witches in Act 1, Scene 3.
What do you think this reveals about their characters?

4) How does Macduff's character contrast with Macbeth's?
Give some examples from the play.

5) Do you think that it's the Witches' fault that Macbeth kills Duncan? Explain your answer.

Practice Questions

"Fair is foul, and foul is fair". These Practice Questions are foul *and* unfair but they're better than getting into the exam and not having the faintest idea who Macbeth is. Try these questions out and if you're a bit hazy on the details of any of the characters, flick back through the section and remind yourself who's who.

Exam-style Question

1 Answer **both** parts **(a)** and **(b)**.

a) How does Shakespeare present Lady Macbeth's thoughts and feelings in the extract below?

b) How does Shakespeare present Lady Macbeth's thoughts and feelings in another part of the play?

Lady Macbeth: Come, you spirits
That tend on mortal thoughts, unsex me here
And fill me from the crown to the toe topfull
Of direst cruelty; make thick my blood,
Stop up th'access and passage to remorse
That no compunctious visitings of nature
Shake my fell purpose nor keep peace between
Th'effect and it. Come to my woman's breasts
And take my milk for gall, you murd'ring ministers,
Wherever in your sightless substances
You wait on nature's mischief.
(Act 1, Scene 5, 38-48)

Controlled Assessment-style Questions

1 Explore how the characters of Macbeth and Macduff are used to present conflict in the play.

2 Show how Shakespeare develops the character of Lady Macbeth in the play.

3 Explore how Shakespeare portrays the characters of Malcolm and Banquo.

Ambition

When I was little, my mum used to say that "'I want' doesn't get". If Macbeth had heard this, he'd probably respond, "'I want' does get, especially if you kill everyone standing in your way". Bad man.

*Ambition is the **Main Theme** in 'Macbeth'*

1) Ambition motivates Macbeth to commit terrible deeds. It changes him from a "valiant" soldier to a "dead butcher".
2) The play shows that ambition is dangerous because it can quickly spiral out of control. Macbeth considers the morality of killing Duncan for a long time but doesn't hesitate about killing Banquo.
3) Once Macbeth starts killing, he has to kill more people to get what he wants and to try and make his position secure. It shows that ambition can make people ruthless and selfish.
4) Both Macbeth and Lady Macbeth are eventually destroyed by their ambition, so the play can be read as a warning against ambition that isn't balanced by reason or morals.

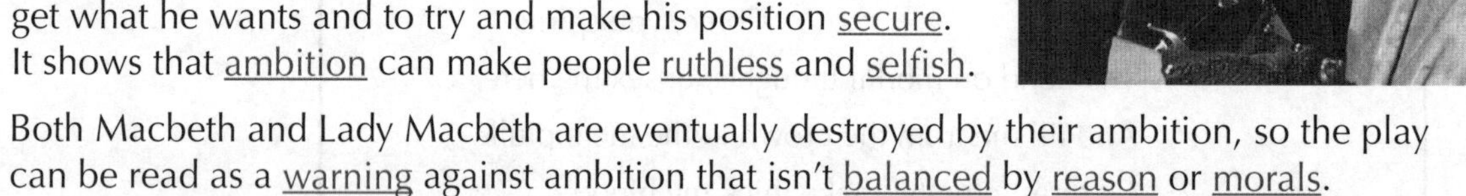

Ambition** is Macbeth's **Biggest Weakness

Context — Tragedy

In Shakespeare's tragedies, the hero is usually a noble person with one main character flaw which leads to their downfall. This is their 'fatal flaw'.

1) Ambition is Macbeth's 'fatal flaw'. He's a brave hero at the start — Duncan calls him "noble" and Lady Macbeth says he "wouldst not play false" to get what he wants.

Character — Lady Macbeth

Lady Macbeth sees that there's a difference between being ambitious and acting on ambition. She says that Macbeth is "not without ambition, but without / The illness should attend it". She thinks that Macbeth isn't ruthless enough to take action to get what he wants.

2) Macbeth's reluctance to kill Duncan shows that he's moral, but his actions emphasise how strong his ambition is — his ambition makes him act against his morals.
3) It also makes him act against his better judgement. He knows that ambition often "o'erleaps itself / And falls" — it can lead a person to aim too high so that they fail and lose everything. This foreshadows Macbeth's own tragic downfall. By the end of the play, Macbeth's lost everything and he dies an "abhorrèd tyrant".

Ambition** can be **Good** or **Bad

1) Not all characters are corrupted by their ambition, as Macbeth and Lady Macbeth are. Ambition can be a positive thing if it's motivated by a desire to help others rather than yourself.
2) Malcolm and Macduff are ambitious for their country. They want to take Macbeth's power away from him, not for their own selfish desires, but for the good of Scotland.
3) Banquo is ambitious for his sons once he's heard the Witches' prophecy. He wants them to be kings, but he doesn't act on the predictions in the violent way that Macbeth does.

I'm ambitious for a piece of cake and a nap...

Ambition isn't always a bad thing — ambition (and cake) in moderation can help people do great things like pass their English exams or write scorching essays. It's when ambition snowballs out of control that the problems mount up...

Loyalty and Betrayal

In general, humans aren't known for their loyalty — golden retrievers, on the other hand, are always loyal. If only Macbeth had been a Macspaniel or a Macpoodle, the story might have ended differently...

*Characters show **Loyalty** through their **Actions***

1) There's a difference between characters who say that they are loyal (like Macbeth, who talks about the "loyalty" he owes to Duncan even when he's plotting to kill him) and characters whose actions show their loyalty (like Macduff). The characters in *Macbeth* show loyalty to different things:

Country

Macduff is loyal to Scotland. He chooses to go to England to ask Malcolm to defend his country instead of protecting his family. He'd rather leave Scotland than see it be ruled by a bad king.

King

The thanes are loyal to Duncan because he's been a "great" king. Macbeth gives Duncan "service and loyalty" by fighting for him in Act 1.

Beliefs

Banquo is loyal to his own sense of honour — he says that he will keep his "allegiance clear". He won't let ambition or the Witches' prophecies affect him.

2) When characters betray their loyalty, it's usually to pursue their own selfish desires.

***Loyalty** is **Rewarded**, **Betrayal** is **Punished**...*

1) Duncan has the old Thane of Cawdor executed for betraying him and rewards Macbeth's loyalty by giving him the title. The play has a circular structure — it ends with Macbeth being killed for betraying Scotland and Malcolm rewarding the thanes' loyalty.

2) Macbeth betrays his own sense of right and wrong. This eventually leads to his loss of self-worth and his death.

3) Betrayal is often linked to power. Power (in the form of titles) can be given or taken away depending on a person's loyalty.

Loyalty and betrayal often go hand in hand, e.g. Macduff's loyalty to Scotland leads him to betray his family.

© Amitava Sarkar

*The Macbeths **Pretend** to be **Loyal***

1) Macbeth is initially loyal to Duncan as "his kinsman and his subject" — this makes it even more shocking when he puts his own desires ahead of his loyalty to the King.

Theme — Reality and Appearances

Lady Macbeth's two-faced nature helps her to betray Duncan — he trusts her as a "Fair and noble hostess" and doesn't see her lust for power.

2) Lady Macbeth fakes an appearance of loyalty. She tells Duncan that she and Macbeth are "Your servants ever", even though they're plotting his murder. It shows how easily she can pretend to be loyal.

3) Shakespeare juxtaposes Lady Macbeth's plotting to kill Duncan with her welcoming him into their castle. This develops her character and makes her murderous intentions more dramatic.

Macbeth has a funny way of showing his loyalty...

If killing someone is a mark of how loyal you are to them, then I'm not interested... betray me all you like. Macbeth's betrayal is made even worse because he seems so loyal at the beginning — it means he had further to fall...

Kingship

When Shakespeare wrote *Macbeth*, kings and queens were properly in charge of running their country — so it was really serious if they were bad people or were bad at the job (*cough* Macbeth).

A King Didn't **Have to Be** the Old King's **Son**

1) In the play, Macbeth suddenly becomes King, even though he's not the heir to the throne. Duncan chooses his eldest son as his heir, but he makes Macbeth next in line after Malcolm and Donalbain.
2) Macbeth wins the throne by killing the King and framing Malcolm and Donalbain. Gradually, other characters realise Macbeth is not a true king.

Historical Context

In Scotland at the time, the successor didn't have to be the King's eldest son, even though it often was.

Malcolm describes **Good** Rulers and **Bad** Rulers

1) Duncan is an example of an ideal king — he's described as "gracious" and inspires loyalty in his subjects, who see him as a "most sainted king" and therefore the rightful ruler of Scotland.
2) In contrast, Macbeth is described as a "tyrant" because he rules selfishly, using violence. He's rarely referred to as "king" which shows that the other characters don't accept him as the true King.
3) In Act 4, Scene 3 Malcolm describes good and bad kings:

Writer's Techniques

Under Duncan's rightful reign, the country is ordered and peaceful. Macbeth's unlawful reign is reflected in the overturned natural order, e.g. day turns to night and horses eat each other.

A bad king is...

bloody,
Luxurious, avaricious, false, deceitful,
Sudden, malicious, smacking of every sin
That has a name.

Malcolm's describing Macbeth's reign here — he's "avaricious" because he's motivated by selfish greed. His lies make him "false" and "deceitful", and he's "bloody" because he uses violence to keep control over his people.

A good king has...

king-becoming graces,
As justice, verity, temperance, stableness,
Bounty, perseverance, mercy, lowliness,
Devotion, patience, courage, fortitude

Malcolm could be describing Duncan in this speech — Duncan shows "temperance" in his calm, peaceful manner, "lowliness" (being humble) in his gratefulness for loyalty, "justice" when dealing with those who betray him and "Bounty" in his generosity.

A Good King Should Be **Holy**

1) Malcolm also says that a good ruler is holy — at the time, people believed the King was appointed by God.
2) The King of England, Edward, has a "healing benediction" and uses "holy prayers" to cure sick people. He's surrounded by "blessings" that "speak him full of grace".
3) In contrast, Macbeth is "Devilish" — he commits murder and talks to evil witches. He's not the chosen King.

© Ellie Kurtz

God bless Kingship and all who sail in her...

The play shows the two extremes of being a ruler — Duncan is a perfect king but Macbeth couldn't be any worse. This makes Macbeth's actions seem more terrible — he's killed a brilliant ruler, then totally messes up the job himself...

Good and Evil

Like so many other stories, the plot of *Macbeth* boils down to a classic case of good versus evil. Obviously you're meant to identify with the 'good' side, unless you're also a murderous crazy person.

*Macbeth is a **Good Man** who does **Evil** acts*

1) At the beginning of the play, Macbeth shows that he's a "noble" person — he has the potential for greatness. Duncan recognises this and makes him Thane of Cawdor.
2) Once he's tempted to give in to his ambition, Macbeth's goodness is overcome by his evil desires. It shows that even good people can be led astray by ambition and power.
3) Macbeth becomes increasingly evil as he becomes hardened to the many crimes he commits.
4) The struggle for the crown of Scotland becomes a battle between good and evil. Macbeth is the evil "tyrant" who must be killed before he destroys Scotland.

© Amitava Sarkar

Shakespeare uses images of darkness to represent evil and images of light to symbolise goodness (see p.56).

Evil** is linked to **Gender

1) Lady Macbeth links cruelty and aggression with masculinity. She wants the spirits to "unsex" her and fill her with "direst cruelty" — she thinks her femininity holds her back from taking violent action.
2) Masculine ideas of evil focus on violence and bloodshed. Though she wants to be more like a man, Lady Macbeth relies on manipulation rather than action. She sees Macbeth's weakness and uses emotional blackmail to persuade him to commit evil.
3) The Witches' gender is ambiguous. Banquo says that they "should be women" but they have beards. Like Lady Macbeth, they rely on manipulation rather than physical force.

Theme — The Supernatural

The supernatural elements of the play are presented as evil and powerful. The Witches are linked to the devil — Banquo calls them "devil" and Macbeth calls them "fiends", which associates them with evil deeds.

Battles** represent the **Conflict** between **Good** and **Evil

1) Shakespeare uses battles to symbolise good and evil.
2) In the opening scene, there's a battle between Scotland and Norway — the enemy army is led by a traitor, "merciless Macdonald", whose "villanies of nature" show that he's evil.
3) The play ends with a battle, this time against Macbeth. Malcolm's men have "dear causes" and fight to "dew the sovereign flower" — in other words, to restore the rightful King. Macbeth is an "abhorrèd tyrant" who represents evil.

Writer's Techniques — Imagery

Shakespeare emphasises the conflict between good and evil through religious imagery — Macbeth is described as "cursèd" and has a name "More hateful" than the devil. In contrast, Young Siward is "God's soldier" because he died fighting to defeat an evil "tyrant".

The good, the bad and the ugly witches...

There's a whole mixture of different characters in the play — some characters are really bad (like the Witches), some are really good (like Duncan) and some (like Macbeth) go from good to bad to worse... to being hated and killed.

The Supernatural

Thrice the stripy zebra danced. Thrice and once the llama pranced. Make the tea and feed the birds. Then sit thee down and read these charmèd words. Ahh, magic...

The *Witches* are a *Supernatural Force*

1) The Witches are an evil supernatural force — their "strange intelligence" and ability to predict the future gives them power over humans. However, when they're planning to harm the sea captain, they say that his ship "cannot be lost", which hints that their power is limited.
2) They're not in many scenes but they drive the action of the play. It's unlikely that Macbeth would have committed so many terrible crimes if he hadn't been influenced by the Witches.

Social Context

At the time Shakespeare was writing, many people thought that witches were real, so the Weïrd Sisters would have seemed believable and frightening to an audience in the 1600s.

Writer's Techniques

The supernatural elements add to the atmosphere — they make the play darker and more frightening. Shakespeare only hints at what's real and what's not, which adds to the drama.

3) The Witches are associated with chaos — they try to impose an unnatural order on what's good and natural. Macbeth says they "untie the winds" and make "castles topple". The Witches are motivated by "destruction" rather than goodness — they represent the struggle between the natural and unnatural order.
4) Shakespeare presents them as completely evil. They are cruel, inhuman and don't show any remorse — in fact, they celebrate evil.

Visions are *Supernatural Signs* of *Guilt*

Macbeth and Lady Macbeth have visions which remind the audience of their terrible guilt:

Act 2, Scene 1 — Macbeth sees a vision of a dagger just as he's about to kill Duncan. It's not clear whether it's leading him to Duncan or warning him against murder. It represents the "bloody business" he's about to do.

Act 3, Scene 4 — Macbeth sees Banquo's ghost, which gives him a "strange infirmity". Nobody else can see the ghost, which suggests that it's a sign of Macbeth's guilty conscience.

Act 5, Scene 1 — Lady Macbeth is driven mad as she imagines that her hands will "ne'er be clean" of Duncan's blood — her guilt is so great that she kills herself.

1) The visions are ambiguous — they could be real or imaginary.
2) The visions fill the characters who see them with fear. Macbeth is "blanched with fear" by Banquo's ghost and his language is agitated and nervous: "Prithee, see there! Behold, look, lo!" His fear has made him lose control of his speech. Macbeth calls his own reaction a "strange infirmity" — it links to other signs of madness later in the play.
3) Lady Macbeth's language when she sleepwalks is desperate, "O, o, o!", and shows that she's disturbed by the vision of blood on her hands. The Doctor says that her heart is "sorely charged" — he sees that the vision is the result of her guilty conscience.

Which Witch is Which — it's difficult to tell...

...although they all have beards, so that certainly helps to make them stand out. The supernatural bits of the play are part of the reason why *Macbeth* is so popular — everyone has an opinion about whether witches and ghosts are real.

Reality and Appearances

There's a big difference between seeming lovely and being lovely. Shakespeare's constantly going on about the difference between appearances and reality in *Macbeth,* so it's worth getting to grips with.

Appearances *can be* ***Deceptive***

1) In *Macbeth*, characters often hide their thoughts and pretend to be something that they're not.
2) Lady Macbeth encourages Macbeth to appear to be good so nobody suspects that he plans to kill Duncan:

> look like th'innocent flower,
> But be the serpent under't
> Act 1, Scene 5

The serpent links Lady Macbeth to Satan who tempted Adam and Eve in the Garden of Eden.

© Ellie Kurtz

3) Macbeth knows that he needs a "False face" to hide his murderous acts. However, when Macbeth sees Banquo's ghost, his face is "the very painting" of his fear and betrays his feelings.
4) At first, Lady Macbeth has no trouble disguising her evil behaviour. She pretends to faint with shock when Duncan's death is discovered. However, her guilt becomes too great to hide and she starts sleepwalking.

People can be deceptive, but the play shows that their true natures come out in the end.

Meanings *of* ***Words*** *are* ***Unclear***

1) The Witches' chant "Fair is foul, and foul is fair" suggests that things that appear good are actually evil.
2) They use language to trick Macbeth and convince him of a false reality — they tell him that "none of woman born" will harm him, which gives him the false confidence to fight to protect his reign.
3) Other characters speak using paradoxes, e.g. Macbeth says, "Nothing is / But what is not". These paradoxes create uncertainty — they show that nobody can tell what's real.

Some characters ***Trust Too Much*** *in* ***Appearances***

1) In a world full of deception and lies, characters suffer when they trust in appearances too much.
2) Duncan trusts Macbeth and dies for it, even though he made the same mistake by trusting the disloyal Thane of Cawdor. When this happens, Duncan says, "There's no art / To find the mind's construction in the face" — he thinks that there's no way of telling what someone's really like.
3) Macbeth knows that reality and appearances don't always match up, but he completely trusts the Witches' prophecies. This leads to his downfall.
4) In contrast, Malcolm is immediately sceptical that Duncan was murdered by his servants and suspects one of the thanes: "To show an unfelt sorrow is an office / Which the false man does easy". His awareness of what "false" men can do causes him to flee and probably saves his life.

> Apparitions and visions seem real to the characters who see them, but they're a sign that the character can't tell reality from appearance.

These pages could be real or just a vision of revision...

It's difficult for the characters in *Macbeth* to tell appearance and reality apart sometimes — it's because so many characters aren't what they seem. Poor Duncan believes that everything he sees is real, and pays the price...

Fate and Free Will

It would be great to see into the future — you'd never be caught without an umbrella and you'd know what exam questions to expect. It would remove the element of surprise though, and that's half the fun...

Fate is the Opposite of Free Will

© Amitava Sarkar

1) Fate is the idea that everything has already been decided, so people can't change what happens to them.
2) Free will means that humans choose their own course of action, so their future is made up of the results of their choices.
3) If it's fate that everything that happens was destined, then it's not Macbeth's fault that he murders Duncan. If free will exists, then Macbeth's own choices lead to his downfall.
4) The play raises a lot of questions, but Shakespeare doesn't make it clear whether it's Macbeth's fate to kill Duncan.

You could say that Macbeth is Doomed from the Start...

1) At times, Macbeth seems to believe in fate. After he hears the Witches' prophecy, he seems happy to let fate take its course — he believes that "chance may crown me, / Without my stir" so he'll become King without doing anything to make it happen.

Characters — The Witches

It's not clear whether the Witches are messengers of Macbeth's fate or whether their prediction inspires Macbeth to make bad choices.

Character — Macbeth

You could say that Macbeth is doomed because of his 'fatal flaw' (see p.38). If he wasn't so ambitious, he'd ignore the Witches and Lady Macbeth.

2) Lady Macbeth thinks that Macbeth is fated to be King — "fate and metaphysical aid doth seem / To have thee crowned withal". Despite believing in fate, she decides Macbeth must act to make it happen.
3) By the end of the play, Macbeth says that life is "a poor player / That struts and frets his hour upon the stage". He feels that people are no more than actors playing a part who aren't in control of their lives.

...or that he Acts out of his own Free Will

1) At first, Macbeth makes a deliberate choice not to kill Duncan after he's considered the options: "We will proceed no further". He carefully weighs up the pros and cons, which suggests that he's in control.
2) Later, Macbeth acts on the Witches' prophecies despite Banquo's earlier warning that they're "instruments of darkness". Macbeth could do as Banquo does and accept the prophecies without acting.
3) Some of the prophecies are self-fulfilling — Macbeth only acts because he hears his future, so he causes it to happen. This suggests that he has free will.

Character — Macbeth

The captain says that Macbeth was "Disdaining fortune" when he fought Macdonald — it shows that Macbeth killed Macdonald against the odds. It hints that Macbeth could have changed his actions if he'd wanted to.

It's your fate to learn the stuff on this page...

...but you can use your free will to take the stuff you've learnt and turn it into sparkling after-dinner conversation to impress your friends and family. There's nothing like a philosophical debate about Shakespeare to keep people awake.

Practice Questions

The themes are like the jammy layer in a sponge cake — they help to stick everything together and stop the play from falling apart in a soggy mess. Jam comes in lots of different flavours, just like themes — strawberry, apricot, raspberry... free will, ambition, good and evil. Try these questions out to see whether you've really got to grips with the themes in *Macbeth*, and if you know all the answers, reward yourself with some cake.

Quick Questions

1) What is Macbeth's biggest weakness?
2) How does Macduff show his loyalty to Scotland?
3) Describe a part of the play when a character betrays something or someone.
4) Name three characteristics that Duncan has that make him a good king.
5) Give three qualities that make a bad ruler in the play.
6) Why does Lady Macbeth want the spirits to "unsex" her?
7) How does Macbeth react to seeing Banquo's ghost?
8) Give an example of a time when Lady Macbeth disguises her evil thoughts or actions.
9) Briefly explain the difference between fate and free will.

In-depth Questions

1) Who do you think is the most loyal character in the play and why?
2) Compare the way that Duncan and Macbeth rule Scotland and explain which of them you think is the more successful ruler.
3) Who do you think is more evil — Macbeth or Lady Macbeth? Why?
4) How does Shakespeare use the Witches to show that appearances can be deceptive?
5) How important is the role of fate in the plot of *Macbeth*?

Practice Questions

Context and Themes — it's one hefty section, but it's worth learning. You can look at lots of these themes from different points of view, so make sure you know them inside out — it'll help you write a balanced essay. Use the questions below to make sure you know your stuff...

Exam-style Questions

1 Answer **both** parts **(a)** and **(b)**.

a) How does Shakespeare present the supernatural in the extract below?

b) How does Shakespeare present the supernatural at another point in the play?

Banquo: you should be women,
And yet your beards forbid me to interpret
That you are so.
Macbeth: Speak, if you can: what are you?
1st Witch: All hail Macbeth! Hail to thee, Thane of Glamis.
2nd Witch: All hail Macbeth! Hail to thee, Thane of Cawdor.
3rd Witch: All hail Macbeth that shalt be King hereafter!
Banquo: Good sir, why do you start, and seem to fear
Things that do sound so fair? I'th'name of truth
Are ye fantastical, or that indeed
Which outwardly ye show? My noble partner
You greet with present grace and great prediction
Of noble having and of royal hope
That he seems rapt withal. To me you speak not.
If you can look into the seeds of time
And say which grain will grow and which will not,
Speak then to me, who neither beg nor fear
Your favours not your hate.

(Act 1, Scene 3, 44-60)

Controlled Assessment-style Questions

1 How are ideas of fate and free will presented in *Macbeth*?

2 Discuss how Shakespeare presents the dangers of ambition in the play.

3 How does Shakespeare explore ideas of loyalty and betrayal in *Macbeth*?

The Structure of 'Macbeth'

Structure is one of the most important parts of a play. Structure is the skill of writing a play so all the bits fit together, in the right order, in a way that works on stage. Shakespeare's structure was the cat's bananas.

A play's **Structure** *is the* **Way** *it's* **Put Together**

1) One of the most important parts of stagecraft is the structure of the play. The structure is the overall design of the play — how the plot is revealed, what events happen when, which scenes focus on thoughts and feelings, and which scenes build towards a dramatic climax.
2) Shakespeare didn't put the scenes in a random order — he had reasons to structure them a certain way:

To Emphasise Important Themes

He introduces the Witches right at the beginning in Act 1, Scene 1. That way the audience knows that there are supernatural forces at work.

To Set the Mood

The first scene of each act sets the mood for the rest of the act. E.g. in Act 2, Scene 1, Macbeth goes to murder Duncan. This sets the dark atmosphere for the whole of Act 2.

Tragedies *have a* **Set Structure**

1) *Macbeth* is a typical tragedy. The first part builds up to the turning point (Duncan's murder), and the second part deals with the consequences of this, which lead to the main character's downfall.
2) The structure helps Shakespeare develop the characters — Macbeth starts off as an honourable, moral character, but he's corrupted by ambition (his fatal flaw). In contrast, Lady Macbeth starts out cruel and remorseless, but she eventually goes mad from guilt.
3) *Macbeth* also has a circular structure — it starts and ends with a battle to defeat a "merciless tyrant". This shows that the events have come full circle and order is restored at the end of the play.

© COLUMBIA / THE KOBAL COLLECTION

Shakespeare **Varies** *the* **Length** *of the* **Scenes**

1) Shakespeare uses short scenes to speed up the action and make the play more exciting.
   - For example, Act 5 is made up of nine short scenes — and a lot happens in this act. Lady Macbeth goes mad, the English army arrives, Lady Macbeth kills herself, Macbeth sees Birnam Wood on the move, Macbeth kills Young Siward, Macduff kills Macbeth and Malcolm becomes King. Phew.
2) Long scenes let Shakespeare explore his characters' emotions and reveal their true characters.
   - In Act 4, Scene 3, Malcolm tests Macduff by claiming to be unfit to be King. Macduff's reaction shows that he is loyal to Malcolm and passionate about his country. Later in that scene, Macduff learns that his wife and children are dead — his grief shows that he cares about his family too.

Stagecraft — ships that prompt in the night...

Shakespeare didn't want people getting bored — or finding the scary and tragic bits funny. He had to use every trick he knew to make the audience jump, cry and give him their money. Sweet smiles with a threatening glint work for me.

The Structure of 'Macbeth'

Shakespeare knew all the tricks to keep the audience from yawning. His favourite tactic — let the audience know that juicy scenes are coming up, without giving away what's going to happen. Easy when you know how.

*Shakespeare **Prepares** you for what's **Going** to **Happen***

Hinting at what's going to happen later on in a play is a good way of keeping the audience on the edge of their seats. Shakespeare does it a lot in *Macbeth*, especially near the start.

1) In Act 1, Scene 1 the Witches let the audience know that they're evil ("Fair is foul") and that they're going to meet Macbeth. This creates dramatic tension because it makes the audience wonder who Macbeth is and what the Witches are planning for him.
2) In Act 1, Scene 3 the Witches tell Macbeth he'll be King, which plants the idea in both Macbeth's and the audience's minds and creates anticipation.
3) In Act 1, Scene 4 Macbeth hears that Malcolm is heir to the throne, not him — this suggests that for the Witches' prophecy to come true, Macbeth will have to do something. The audience starts to wonder what Macbeth's capable of, and how strong his ambition is.

© BRITISH LION / THE KOBAL COLLECTION / BOULTON, DAVIS

4) The apparitions' prophecies in Act 4, Scene 1 hint at things to come. The audience suspects the prophecies will come true, but doesn't know how, which builds suspense.

Theme — Supernatural

The supernatural elements in the play (the Witches, the apparitions, Macbeth's vision of a dagger and Banquo's ghost) create tension. They make things seem uncertain and evil.

***Suspense** — what will happen next?*

Shakespeare leaves the audience in little doubt it's going to be a tragedy — but he still keeps a few questions open about what's going to happen.

Act 1, Scene 7 Macbeth battles with his conscience before killing Duncan.	Will he go through with it? We don't find out until Act 2.
Act 3, Scene 1 Banquo suspects that Macbeth killed Duncan. Macbeth plots to kill Banquo.	Will Banquo accuse Macbeth? Will Macbeth kill Banquo before he gets the chance? We don't find out until later in Act 3.
Act 4, Scene 3 Macduff learns that his family have been murdered and vows to take revenge on Macbeth.	Will Macduff kill Macbeth? We don't find out until Act 5.
Act 5 The scenes alternate between Macbeth preparing for battle and the English army advancing.	Who will win? What will happen to Macbeth? We don't find out until the end of the play.

The Structure of 'Macbeth'

Macbeth is made up of key scenes and minor scenes. It's not full-on murder and witches all the way through — but every bit is there for a reason and scenes can have lots of different purposes.

*The **First Part** is structured around Macbeth's **Rise to Power***

Key Scenes In Acts 1 and 2 the key scenes are focused on Macbeth becoming King. The plot gradually builds up until the murder of Duncan is discovered and Macbeth is crowned.

Act 1

Scene 3
Macbeth meets the Witches, who tell him he'll be King.

Scene 7
Lady Macbeth persuades Macbeth to kill Duncan.

Act 2

Scene 1
Macbeth goes to kill Duncan.

Scene 3
Macduff finds Duncan's body.

Act 1, Scene 1
The Witches are introduced.

Act 1, Scene 2
Duncan talks about the battle.

Act 1, Scene 4
Macbeth starts to think about killing Duncan.

Act 1, Scenes 5&6
Lady Macbeth learns of the Witches' prophecy. Duncan arrives at Macbeth's castle.

Act 2, Scene 2
Lady Macbeth covers up the murder.

Act 2, Scene 4
An old man talks about weird events. Macbeth is crowned.

Minor Scenes The minor scenes build up the tension and delay the actual murder.

*In the **Second Part**, things **Fall Apart** for Macbeth*

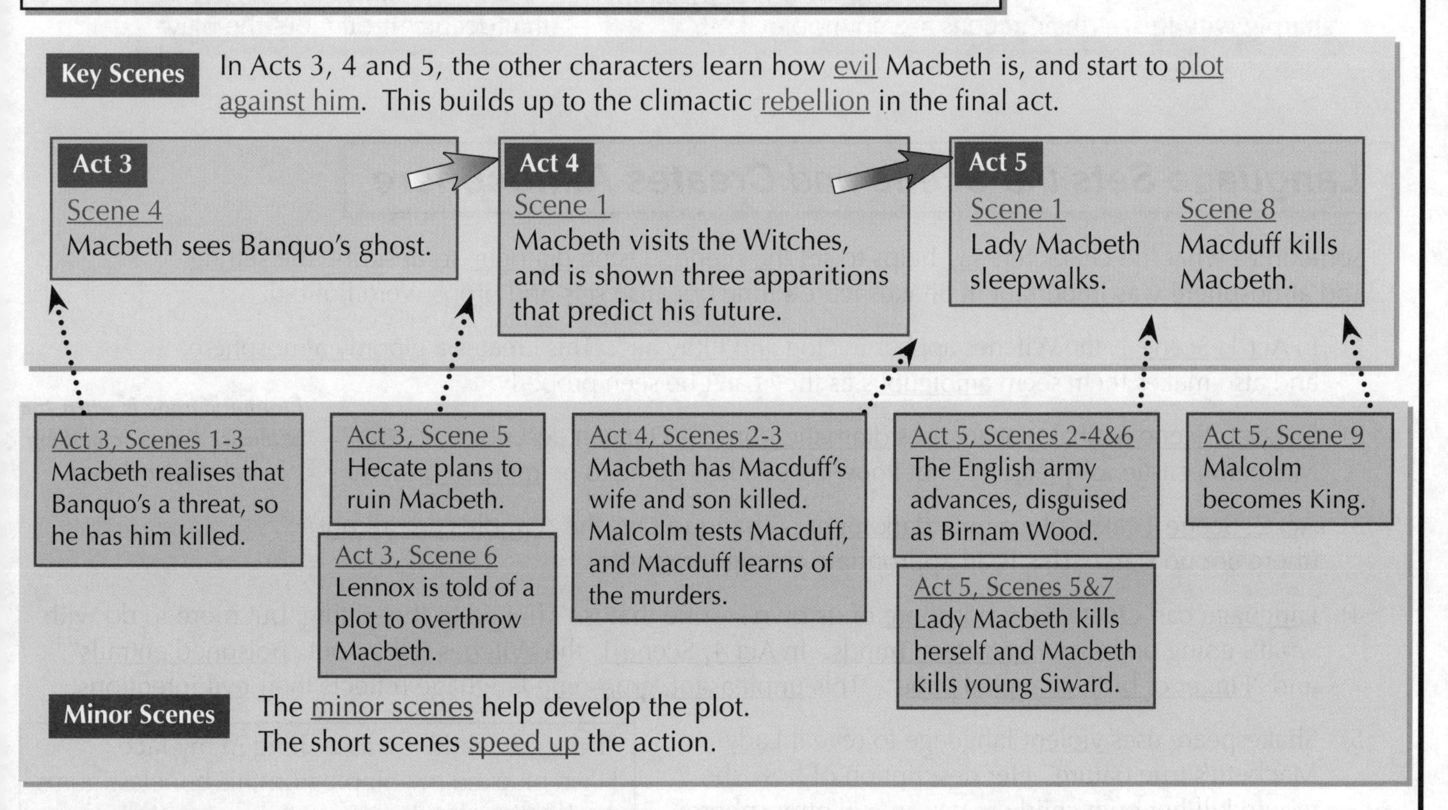

Is that a dagger I see before me — no dear, it's a potato peeler...

If you're writing about structure, I'd suggest focusing on key scenes — the ones where tragedy and murder are at their peak. It's fine to discuss minor scenes too — but don't make them the main subject (unless the question mentions them).

Mood and Atmosphere

Horror, revenge and suspense — *Macbeth* certainly ain't your average slushy romance. Shakespeare keeps the mood pretty dark almost all the way through the play — there's not much in the way of light relief.

*Shakespeare creates **Atmosphere** in **Different Ways***

Shakespeare uses different methods to create different atmospheres, which are an important part of the play. Some of the techniques he uses are:

- Setting
- Use of the supernatural
- Humour
- Different senses
- Language

In particular, imagery helps to create different moods — see pages 55-57.

Different Settings** Create Different **Moods

Shakespeare chose the settings of his scenes very carefully — they add to the atmosphere of the play.

The Witches always appear in a spooky setting, usually in deserted places. This gives a sense of isolation and secrecy, and highlights the fact that they are separated from the rest of the characters. They are often accompanied by "thunder and lightning", which makes them seem menacing — this is an example of pathetic fallacy. Each apparition is introduced with more "thunder", so they appear threatening.

Pathetic fallacy is when an object, weather or setting reflects the mood or characters' emotions.

A lot of the scenes take place in and around Macbeth's castles in Scotland. This reminds the audience that the Macbeths are noble. However, the way they act contrasts sharply with this — their actions are not noble at all.

Most of Act 5 takes place as Malcolm's army advances, which highlights the violence that occurs throughout the play.

Language Sets** the **Scene** and **Creates Atmosphere

Sometimes what the characters say helps to set the scene. Using dialogue to describe the setting and atmosphere was important in Shakespeare's time because sets and props were limited.

1) In Act 1, Scene 1, the Witches appear in "fog and filthy air". This creates a gloomy atmosphere, and also makes them seem ambiguous as they can't be seen properly.
2) In Act 1, Scene 6, Shakespeare uses dramatic irony — Duncan describes Macbeth's castle as "pleasant", not knowing that he's going to be murdered there.

Dramatic irony is when the audience knows something a character doesn't.

3) Act 2, Scene 1 takes place on a dark night — Banquo says the "candles are all out" (there are no stars). This is an appropriate setting for murder.
4) Language can create an atmosphere of its own — one that isn't linked to the setting, but more to do with what's going on in the characters' minds. In Act 4, Scene 1, the Witches talk about "poisoned entrails", and "Finger of birth-strangled babe". This unpleasant, gruesome language reflects their evil intentions.
5) Shakespeare uses violent language to reveal Lady Macbeth's true nature. Her description of how she would kill her own child creates an evil atmosphere:
6) He also uses short lines of dialogue, questions and exclamations to create feelings of panic and confusion.

"I would, while it was smiling in my face,
Have plucked my nipple from his boneless gums
And dashed the brains out"
Act 1, Scene 7

Mood and Atmosphere

Shakespeare *uses the* ***Senses*** *to set the scene*

By making the characters describe what they can see or hear, Shakespeare makes the scenes more vivid — it helps the audience imagine what's happening, especially as there wouldn't have been many props.

1) When Macduff has just discovered Duncan's body, he says it will "destroy your sight / With a new Gorgon". This emphasises the horror of the discovery — he feels he's gone blind from seeing something so terrible.
2) Earlier in the play, Duncan's arrival is introduced by a "Flourish" (or fanfare). This contrasts with the "hideous trumpet" and "alarum bell" that announce his death, and shows how the atmosphere has changed.
3) On the night of Duncan's murder, Lennox hears "strange screams of death", which create a dark, frightening atmosphere.
4) The army approaches to the sound of a "Drum". The sounds of battle highlight the violence that happens throughout the play.

Writer's Techniques

These noises contrast with the moments of silence — e.g. the quiet calm when everyone's sleeping, just before Macbeth murders Duncan.

Unnatural *and* ***Supernatural Events*** *create* ***Tension***

1) Seemingly supernatural events, such as the dagger Macbeth sees and Banquo's ghost, create a tense, uneasy atmosphere. It's uncomfortable because it's not clear if these visions exist or if Macbeth is going mad.
2) After Duncan's murder, there are a number of "unnatural" events, e.g. horses eating each other and day turning to "dark night". This creates a troubled atmosphere, because the natural order has been disturbed.
3) Every appearance of the Witches has a dark, spooky atmosphere. It's not just the setting that creates this mood (see p. 50) — their "imperfect" speech and "Filthy" appearance add to the atmosphere.

The ***Porter*** *provides* ***Light Relief*** *— but also* ***Increases*** *the* ***Tension***

1) One of the few bits of comedy in the play comes in Act 2, Scene 3, when a drunken Porter rambles for a bit. This comic interlude delays the discovery of Duncan's body, which increases the tension.
2) Even here the atmosphere is dark — the Porter talks about "hell" and "Beelzebub" (the devil). He refers to Macbeth's castle as "hell-gate" and calls himself a "devil-porter". This suggests that the visitors are entering hell to be greeted by the devil (Macbeth).
3) Shakespeare also gives the audience a bit of light relief in Act 4, Scene 2, when Lady Macduff and her son chat and joke. However, their jokes are dark and touch on serious subjects: "there are liars and swearers enow to beat the honest men and hang up them." Since Macbeth ordered their murder in the previous scene, their banter also increases the audience's suspense.

I played a tree in my school production of 'Macbeth'...

The settings are really important to the play — but they can be interpreted in different ways. Directors can choose to set it wherever they want — productions set in the present day probably wouldn't use many castles.

Poetry in Shakespeare

This page is a bit dull and technical, but I haven't just stuck it in to wind you up.
If you know the rules about the poetry, it'll be easier to read and easier to write about. Sigh.

Shakespeare *Mainly* uses *Blank Verse*

1) Blank verse is a type of poetry that follows these three rules:
   - The lines usually don't rhyme.
   - Each line has 10 or 11 syllables.
   - Each line has 5 big beats.

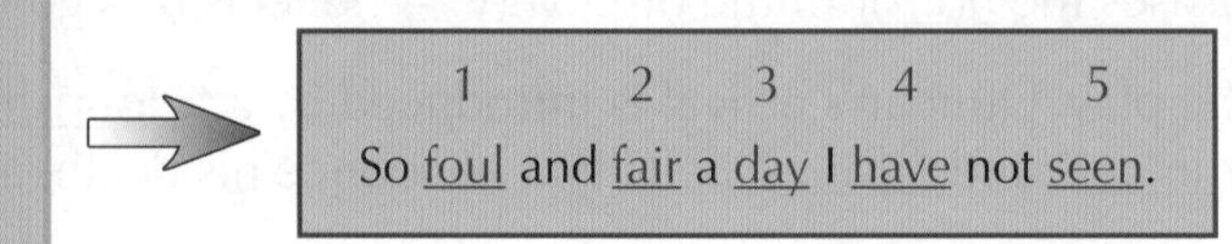

2) Even in short, choppy bits of conversation Shakespeare usually sticks to five big beats a line. The words are staggered to show that they're all part of one line of poetry:

> 1 2 3 4 5
> MACBETH: Your children shall be kings.
> BANQUO: You shall be King.

3) For serious and important bits the rhythm is regular. Most of the characters are lords, and they nearly always talk in this regular rhythm — it makes them sound posh:

> 1 2 3 4 5
> Thou hast it now – King, Cawdor, Glamis, all

4) The Porter, like most lower-class characters, talks in prose and without much set rhythm. This sets him apart from the upper-class characters and makes his speech sound more natural.

5) Lady Macbeth talks in prose when she sleepwalks — her madness has made her lose control.

The *Witches* always speak in *Rhyme*

1) The Witches speak in a different way to the other characters:
   - They speak in rhyme — usually rhyming couplets.
   - Each line has 7 or 8 syllables.
   - Each line has 4 big beats.

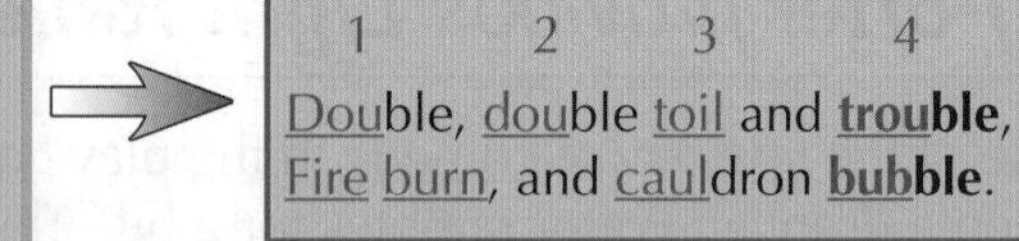

2) The way they speak emphasises the fact that they are different to the other characters — they exist outside the natural order of the world, so they speak unnaturally.

3) In Act 4, Scene 1, the rhyme and rhythm they use make their speech sound like a chant — this is appropriate, as they are casting a spell.

4) Hecate and the apparitions speak in the same way — this links them to the Witches, and shows that they are supernatural too.

5) Some of the other characters like Macbeth and Lady Macbeth occasionally speak in rhyme — usually to make two lines of speech sound more final or to emphasise that it's important:

> MACBETH: Hear it not; Duncan, for it is a **knell**
> That summons thee to heaven or to **hell**.
> Act 2, Scene 1

Poetry in Shakespeare

Shakespeare changes the *Pace*

1) Long words and sentences slow things down.
For example, in this bit Macbeth sounds thoughtful:

> "My thought, whose murder yet is but fantastical,
> Shakes so my single state of man that function
> Is smothered in surmise, and nothing is,
> But what is not."
> Act 1, Scene 3

> "All my pretty ones?
> Did you say all? O hell-kite! All?"
> Act 4, Scene 3

2) Short words and sentences speed things up. Here Shakespeare does this to make Macduff sound upset.

Shakespeare uses *Different Rhythms* to show *Different Emotions*

1) Shakespeare often changes the rhythm of lines by messing around with the punctuation and choice of words.

2) This bit's got a steady rhythm. Duncan's making small talk with Banquo.

> "This castle hath a pleasant seat; the air
> Nimbly and sweetly recommends itself
> Unto our gentle senses."
> Act 1, Scene 6

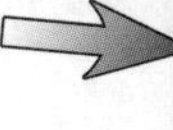

3) Here, the punctuation's very choppy and the rhythm's all over the place. Macbeth has just seen Banquo's ghost — the rhythm and short words show that he's scared and tense. His questions show his uncertainty and disbelief.

> "Why do you show me this? — A fourth? Start, eyes!
> What, will the line stretch out to th'crack of doom?"
> Act 4, Scene 1

Word Order Emphasises different words

1) Shakespeare changes the word order to make important words stand out more.

> "Macduff was from his mother's womb
> Untimely ripped."
> Act 5, Scene 8

2) The natural way to say this would be:
"Macduff was untimely ripped from his mother's womb."

3) Having "Untimely ripped" at the end of the sentence makes it more dramatic. The whole sentence builds tension by saving the key information until the end.

Soliloquies show the *Characters' Thoughts* and *Feelings*

1) A soliloquy is a long speech by one character that is not spoken to any other character on stage.

2) It's just them thinking out loud about their emotions, so it's a good way of showing the audience how a character is honestly feeling.

Some Important Soliloquies in *Macbeth*:

- Lady Macbeth's speech to the spirits in Act 1, Scene 5.
- Macbeth's speech about killing Duncan, in Act 1, Scene 7.
- Macbeth seeing the dagger just before he kills Duncan in Act 2, Scene 1.

There are lots more examples of soliloquies in Macbeth, these are just a few to get you started.

Shakespeare was a poet — but did he know it...

Don't just describe what poetry is used — always write about how Shakespeare uses poetry to create different effects.

Puns and Wordplay

Shakespeare used a lot of puns (using words that look or sound the same but have different meanings). Sometimes the characters make deliberate puns, but at other times they don't seem to do it on purpose.

There are **Puns** everywhere

1) Shakespeare loved puns — his plays are full of them. They were really popular at the time he was writing.
2) Sometimes they're funny (though it's often very dark humour), and sometimes it's just clever wordplay.

> MALCOLM: There's **warrant** in that theft
> Which **steals** itself when there's no mercy left.
> Act 2, Scene 3

"Warrant" can mean either "justification" or "arrest warrant".

"Steal" can mean either "to sneak" or "to thieve".

3) The double meanings of both "warrant" and "steal" reveal why Malcolm and Donalbain's actions could be viewed as suspicious. They are running away because they fear for their lives, but it could be interpreted as running away out of guilt.
4) Shakespeare uses puns to reveal what characters are thinking. In this example, Lady Macbeth isn't making a deliberate pun — she's using "crown" to mean head, but it shows her desire to become Queen is always on her mind.

> LADY MACBETH: And fill me from the **crown** to the toe topfull
> Of direst cruelty
> Act 1, Scene 5

Shakespeare uses **Wordplay** to create **Dramatic Irony**

1) Dramatic irony is when the audience knows something the characters on stage don't — for example, Macduff describes Lady Macbeth as "gentle" and says that the news of Duncan's murder would "murder" her. This is dramatic irony because the audience knows that Lady Macbeth has planned Duncan's murder.
2) In Act 2, Scene 3, the Porter's wordplay creates dramatic irony. He jokingly refers to Macbeth's castle as "hell-gate" and talks about someone who is sent to hell for committing "treason" — the audience knows that Macbeth has committed treason by killing the King, so the Porter's words are truer than he knows.

Some characters **Contradict** themselves

An oxymoron is where two words contradict each other. A paradox is a statement that contradicts itself or cancels itself out.

1) Shakespeare uses paradoxes and oxymorons to heighten the tension.

© Ellie Kurtz

2) The Witches' predictions are ambiguous. The things they predict seem impossible, and yet they come true. Macbeth describes their words as "lies like truth" — this is an oxymoron because lies are never truthful.
3) The Witches often speak in paradoxes — "When the battle's lost and won". This makes them very ambiguous — the audience doesn't know what their motives are, or whether they can be trusted.

Theme — Reality and Appearances

All these puns and paradoxes emphasise that nothing is as it seems, e.g. "Fair is foul, and foul is fair".

Imagery and Symbolism

Macbeth is full of images — they make the language rich and interesting, and help the audience understand the thoughts and feelings of the characters. Of course, they also make the play a bit tricky to study.

There are Three Kinds of Imagery to Look Out For

Imagery helps you picture what Shakespeare's describing, and makes it stick in your mind better.

Similes are when One thing is Like Something else

"I had else been perfect;
Whole as the marble, founded as the rock"
Act 3, Scene 4

1) Macbeth's saying he was solid and grounded, like rock. Rock is firm and fixed, as he was before.

2) Here, Angus compares Macbeth to a "thief", because he's stolen power from Duncan. Angus is saying that Macbeth's responsibilities as King are too much for him, like clothes that are too big for him to fill.

"Now does he feel his title
Hang loose about him, **like a giant's robe
Upon a dwarfish thief.**"
Act 5, Scene 2

A Metaphor is when One thing is said to be Something Else

"There the **grown serpent** lies; the **worm** that's fled
Hath nature that in time will **venom** breed,
No **teeth** for th'present."
Act 3, Scene 4

1) Here, Macbeth describes Banquo as a snake and his son Fleance as a "worm". He still sees Fleance as a threat, and is afraid of his "venom".

2) Snakes and serpents are used as an extended metaphor (a repeated metaphor) throughout the play, usually to describe deception or betrayal. For example, Lady Macbeth tells Macbeth to "look like th'innocent flower / But be the serpent under't".

© Amitava Sarkar

Personification means Describing a thing As If it were a Person

"Life's but a **walking shadow**, a **poor player**
That struts and frets his hour upon the stage
And then is heard no more."
Act 5, Scene 5

1) Here, Macbeth personifies life, comparing it to a "walking shadow" and an actor, whose influence is limited to his time on stage. This shows that Macbeth thinks that life is brief and pointless.

2) Here, the earth is personified as a person with a fever to show that Duncan's death was unnatural.

"the earth
Was **feverous** and did **shake**"
Act 2, Scene 3

Shakespeare's images — homeboy bard, punk bard...

Learn all three types of imagery, and use them in your essays. Maybe even drop them into everyday conversations — that'll be sure to impress. Mind you, arriving at school by abseiling from a helicopter would be more impressive.

Imagery and Symbolism

The main point of imagery is to liven up the language, and make the themes more obvious.

Light *Symbolises* ***Good****,* ***Dark*** *Symbolises* ***Evil***

1) Macbeth and Lady Macbeth both use images of darkness when they talk about evil deeds. They also use darkness to represent blindness and ignorance, and light to represent sight and knowledge.

Theme — Good and Evil

The witches are described as "instruments of darkness", which emphasises the fact that they're evil.

2) Macbeth realises that his intentions are evil — he describes his thoughts as "black".

Images of Darkness

"Stars, hide your fires,
Let not light see my black and deep desires"
Act 1, Scene 4

"Come, thick night,
And pall thee in the dunnest smoke of hell,
That my keen knife see not the wound it makes,
Nor heaven peep through the blanket of the dark"
Act 1, Scene 5

3) The Macbeths want to "hide" their evil thoughts and deeds in darkness — the murder of Duncan takes place on a dark, starless night when the "candles are all out". The darkness highlights how evil Duncan's murder is.

4) This is further reflected by the "strange" and "unnatural" events that take place after his death — "by the clock, 'tis day, / And yet dark night strangles the travelling lamp". This image shows that darkness and evil (Macbeth) have overcome the natural goodness and light (Duncan).

5) Light is associated with goodness — here, Duncan compares his loyal Lords to "stars":

Images of Light

"signs of nobleness, like stars, shall shine"
Act 1, Scene 4

Nature *represents the* ***Correct Order*** *of the world*

1) The way nature behaves shows the state of events — Duncan's murder disrupts the natural order. As well as "night's predominance", horses have "Turned wild in nature" and eaten each other.

2) Duncan's murder is symbolised by the image: "A falcon, towering in her pride of place, / Was by a mousing owl hawked at and killed". It's unnatural for an owl to kill a falcon, so this emphasises the fact that Duncan's murder has disrupted the natural order of things.

3) Plant imagery is used throughout the play — Duncan compares Macbeth and Banquo to plants that he will harvest. This image is continued in Act 5, Scene 2, but now Macbeth is compared to the "weeds" and Malcolm is the "sovereign flower". This contrast shows how corrupt Macbeth has become.

Health *and* ***Disease*** *represent the* ***State*** *of* ***Scotland***

1) Shakespeare uses images of disease and injury to highlight what Scotland is like under Macbeth's rule.

2) Macbeth asks the Doctor to cure Scotland: "find her disease, / And purge it to a sound and pristine health". This is ironic — he can't see that he is Scotland's disease, and the country will only recover when he's dead.

3) Macduff sees Macbeth's reign as causing injury to Scotland.

4) Malcolm is later described as the "med'cine" that will cure Scotland, which reinforces the belief that he is the rightful King.

Images of Wounds

"Bleed, bleed, poor country!"
"It weeps, it bleeds; and each new day a gash
Is added to her wounds."
Act 4, Scene 3

Imagery and Symbolism

*Images of **Blood** and **Water** symbolise **Guilt** and **Innocence***

1) Shakespeare uses images of blood to represent guilt — from the blood-stained daggers that Lady Macbeth plants on Duncan's guards, to the "damned spot" that she imagines on her hands.
2) The image of water is associated with washing away the guilt — Lady Macbeth claims that "A little water clears us of this deed", but Macbeth wonders whether "all great Neptune's ocean" would be enough to wash the blood (and guilt) away.
3) Lady Macbeth's madness shows that she can't get rid of her guilt — she asks, "will these hands ne'er be clean?" Cleanliness is linked to innocence here.

© Amitava Sarkar

Masculinity** represents **Aggression** and **Courage

1) Shakespeare links the idea of masculinity to violence. Lady Macbeth bullies her husband into killing Duncan by questioning his masculinity: "When you durst do it, then you were a man." Macbeth uses the same tactic to persuade the murderers to kill Banquo, saying "in the catalogue ye go for men".
2) Lady Macbeth prays to the spirits to "unsex" her — she wants female qualities like kindness and compassion to be removed. She rejects her maternal instincts, saying "take my milk for gall".
3) We see another side of masculinity when Macduff learns of his family's murder. Malcolm tells him to "Dispute it like a man" (i.e. take revenge), but Macduff says he must "feel it as a man" — he believes men should show compassion too. This makes the audience question whether violence is what makes a man.

Everyday Life** can be **Disrupted** by **Guilt

1) Sleep symbolises a clear conscience — so lack of sleep suggests guilt. For a guilty mind, sleep brings "wicked dreams". After murdering Duncan, Macbeth worries that he'll never be able to sleep again.

> "Methought I heard a voice cry, 'Sleep no more! Macbeth does murder sleep'"
> Act 2, Scene 2

2) Lady Macbeth's sleepwalking in Act 5 is a sign of her guilt — she can no longer sleep peacefully.
3) It is also suggested that Scotland can't eat or sleep — being unable to fulfil these basic needs shows how badly Macbeth's rule has affected the country.

> "Give to our tables meat, sleep to our nights,
> Free from our feasts and banquets bloody knives"
> Act 3, Scene 6

4) Clothing is symbolic too — at first, Macbeth is reluctant to wear the "borrowed robes" of the Thane of Cawdor. Banquo reinforces this, saying that the "New honours" are like "strange garments".

I could do with a nap...

Shakespeare used loads of images for all sorts of reasons, so if your essay's on his use of language make sure you write shedloads on it. In fact, imagery needs at least a mention in most types of essay — go on, you know you want to...

Practice Questions

You need to get Shakespeare's techniques sorted out. It's one of the things the examiners expect you to understand. It's all about how Shakespeare made the play good — well-told, atmospheric and gripping... So answer these questions, and keep going through them until you know the answers. Then you can pass the exam, get a job, become a reality TV star, whatever...

Quick Questions

1) What effect do short scenes have?

2) When does Shakespeare first introduce the supernatural?

3) Find a scene where the mood is:
   a) spooky   b) comic

4) Which characters always speak in rhyme?

5) "We have scotched the snake, not killed it"
   Is this...   a) a simile   b) a metaphor   c) personification?

6) Why does Lady Macbeth want the spirits to "unsex" her?

In-depth Questions

1) Pick a scene in the play and describe how it helps build tension and suspense.

2) Pick a scene in the play and describe how Shakespeare creates a spooky atmosphere.

3) Explain how the Witches' speech is different from that of the other characters.
   What effect does this have?

4) Why do you think Shakespeare makes the Porter speak in prose?

5) Find a metaphor in the play. Explain what the imagery shows, and how it fits with the atmosphere of the rest of the scene.

6) How does Shakespeare use images of light and darkness?

7) a) Which of these types of imagery are used to show guilt?

   i) light   ii) darkness   iii) disease   iv) medicine   v) lack of sleep   vi) food

   b) Why do you think Shakespeare uses so many images for guilt in *Macbeth*?

Practice Questions

Well, enough of that easy-peasy warm-up stuff. Now it's time to show off your sparkling skills of analysis, insight and general fabulousness with these exam-style questions. Enjoy...

Exam-style Questions

1 Answer **both** parts **(a)** and **(b)**.

a) Discuss how Shakespeare presents the idea of masculinity in the extract below.

b) Discuss how Shakespeare presents the idea of masculinity in a different part of the play.

Lady Macbeth:
When you durst do it, then you were a man.
And to be more than what you were, you would
Be so much more the man. Nor time, nor place
Did then adhere, and yet you would make both.
They have made themselves and that their fitness now
Does unmake you. I have given suck and know
How tender 'tis to love the babe that milks me:
I would, while it was smiling in my face,
Have plucked my nipple from his boneless gums
And dashed the brains out, had I so sworn
As you have done to this.

(Act 1, Scene 7, 49-59)

Controlled Assessment-style Questions

1 Explore how Shakespeare uses the structure of *Macbeth* to build tension in the play.

2 Examine how Shakespeare uses language to create atmosphere in *Macbeth*.

3 Write about the ways Shakespeare presents good and evil in *Macbeth*.

Assessment Advice

These pages will help with your exam or Controlled Assessment. In the Controlled Assessment you may have to link the play with other texts, but this section is still worth reading — it shows the kind of detail you should include.

The exam questions will test Three Main Skills

1) Write about the text in a thoughtful way with suitable examples and quotations to back up your points.
2) Identify and explain features of the play's form, structure and language. Show how Shakespeare uses these to present the ideas, themes, characters and settings, and how these affect audiences differently according to the times and societies they live in.
3) Write with good spelling, grammar, punctuation and paragraphing — it'll help you get top marks.

Read the Question Carefully and Underline Key Words

1) In the exam, you'll usually get a choice of two questions and you'll have to pick one.
2) The question will have a Part A and a Part B. Read the question at least twice and underline the key words.

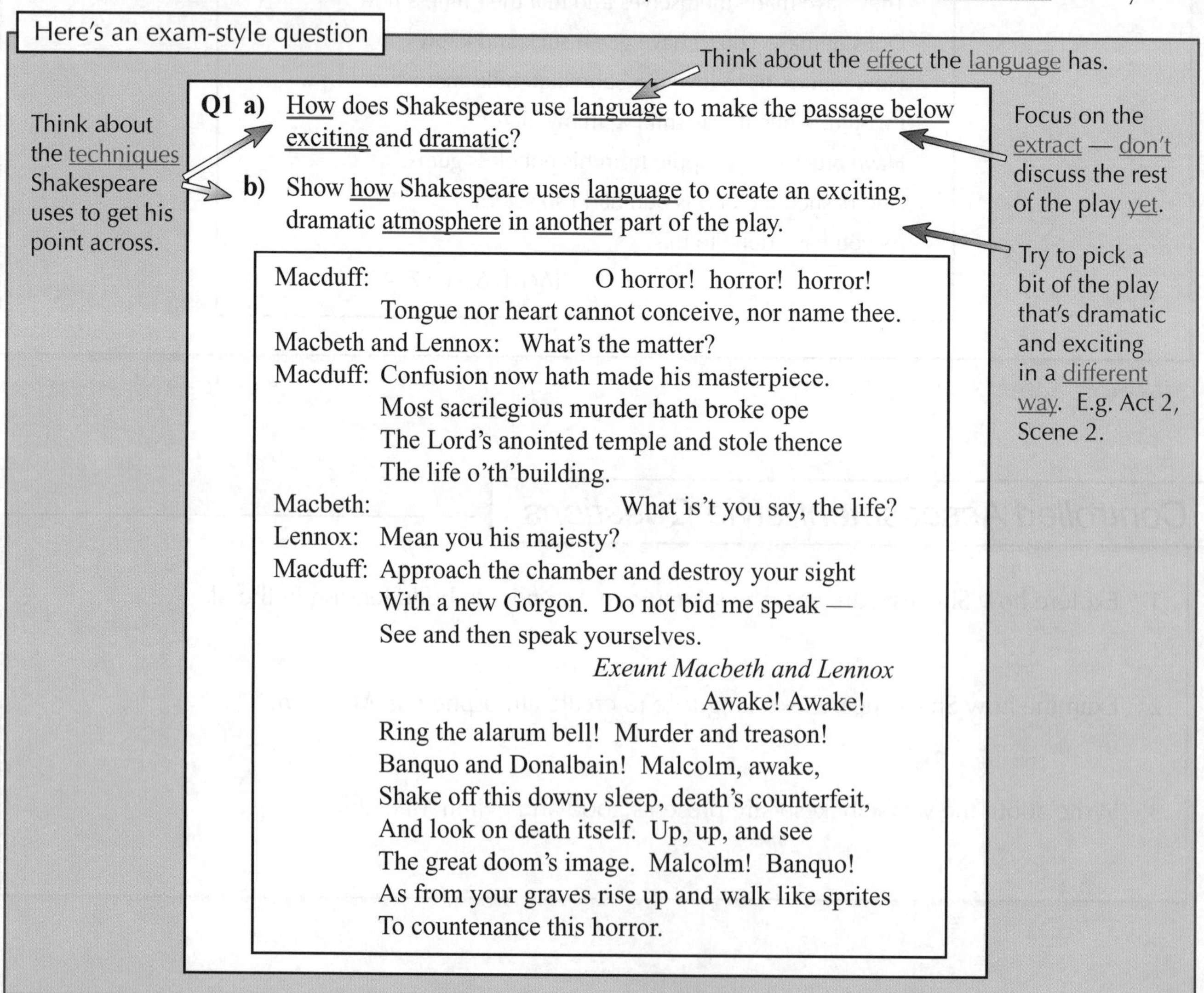

The advice squad — the best cops in the NYPD...

Whatever question you're asked, your answer should touch on the main characters, themes, structure and language.

Structure and Planning

It's easy to panic in the exam — all the more reason to spend five minutes jotting down a cunning plan for what you're going to write. It'll give you time to think and give your answer a better structure.

Plan your answer before you start

1) If you plan, you're less likely to forget something important.
2) Write your plan at the top of your answer booklet and draw a neat line through it when you've finished.
3) Don't spend too long on your plan. It's only rough work, so you don't need to write in full sentences. Here are a few examples of different ways you can plan your answer:

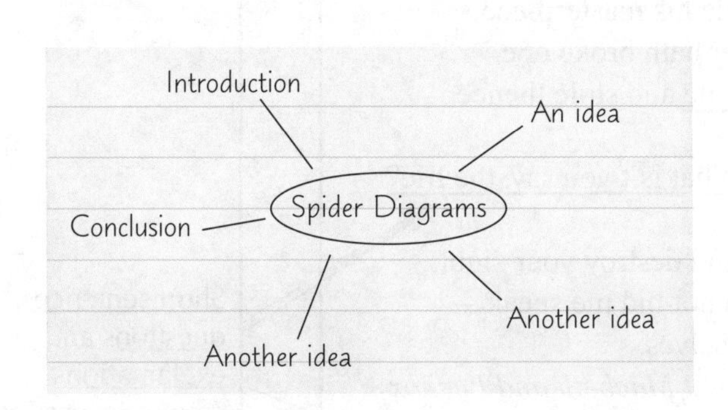

Bullet points and headings...
- Intro...
- An idea...
- The next idea...

Tables with...

A point...	Quote to back this up...
Another point...	Quote...
A different point...	Quote...
A brand new point...	Quote...

4) A good plan will help you organise your ideas — and write a good, well-structured essay.

Structure your answer

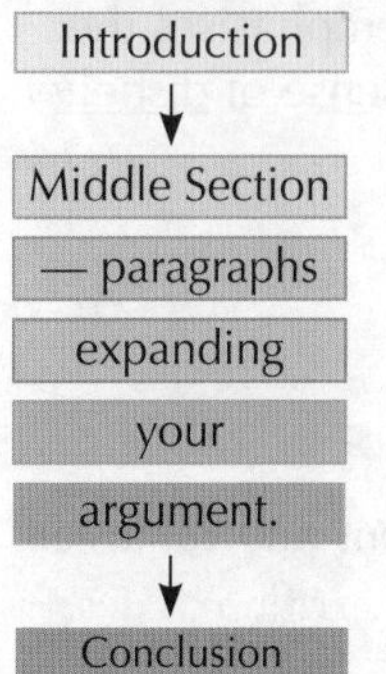

1) Your introduction should give a brief answer to the question you're writing about. Make it clear how you're going to tackle the topic.
2) The middle section of your essay should explain your answer in detail and give evidence to back it up. Write a paragraph for each point you make. Start the paragraph by making the point, then back it up with evidence — examples and quotations from *Macbeth*. Then develop your point by analysing your example or quotation — say why it's important.
3) Don't forget a conclusion — a paragraph at the end which sums up your main points.

Don't Panic if you make a Mistake

1) Okay, so say the exam is going well and you've timed it beautifully. Instead of putting your feet up on the desk for the last 5 minutes, it's a good idea to read through your answers at the end and correct any mistakes...
2) If you want to get rid of something, just cross it out. Don't scribble over it.
3) If you've left stuff out write it in a separate section at the end of the essay. Put a star (*) next to both the extra writing and the place you want it to go.

Dirk never panicked — he was ready for anything.

To plan or not to plan, that is the question...

The answer is yes, yes, a thousand times yes. Don't just dive straight in, worried that planning will take up valuable time. Five minutes spent organising a well-structured answer is loads better than pages of waffle. Mmm waffles.

Sample Exam — Planning Part A

And now the bit you've all been waiting for — a lovely little sample plan for Part A of the question. Enjoy.

Have *Another Look* at the *Extract*...

Read the extract closely and underline the important bits. Think about the language and the punctuation.

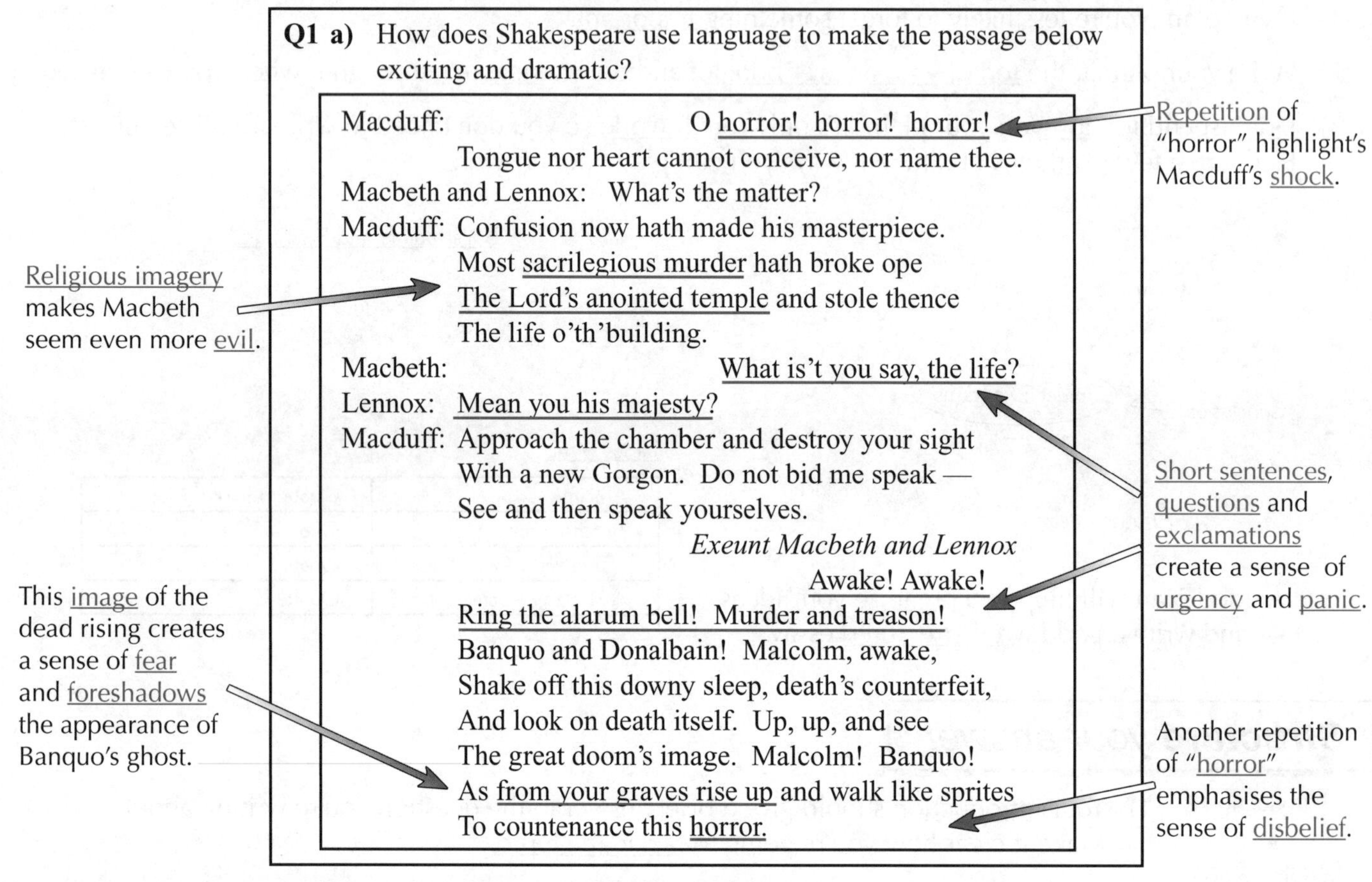

Q1 a) How does Shakespeare use language to make the passage below exciting and dramatic?

Macduff: O horror! horror! horror!
Tongue nor heart cannot conceive, nor name thee.
Macbeth and Lennox: What's the matter?
Macduff: Confusion now hath made his masterpiece.
Most sacrilegious murder hath broke ope
The Lord's anointed temple and stole thence
The life o'th'building.
Macbeth: What is't you say, the life?
Lennox: Mean you his majesty?
Macduff: Approach the chamber and destroy your sight
With a new Gorgon. Do not bid me speak —
See and then speak yourselves.
Exeunt Macbeth and Lennox
Awake! Awake!
Ring the alarum bell! Murder and treason!
Banquo and Donalbain! Malcolm, awake,
Shake off this downy sleep, death's counterfeit,
And look on death itself. Up, up, and see
The great doom's image. Malcolm! Banquo!
As from your graves rise up and walk like sprites
To countenance this horror.

Here's how you could *Plan* your *Answer* for *Part A*...

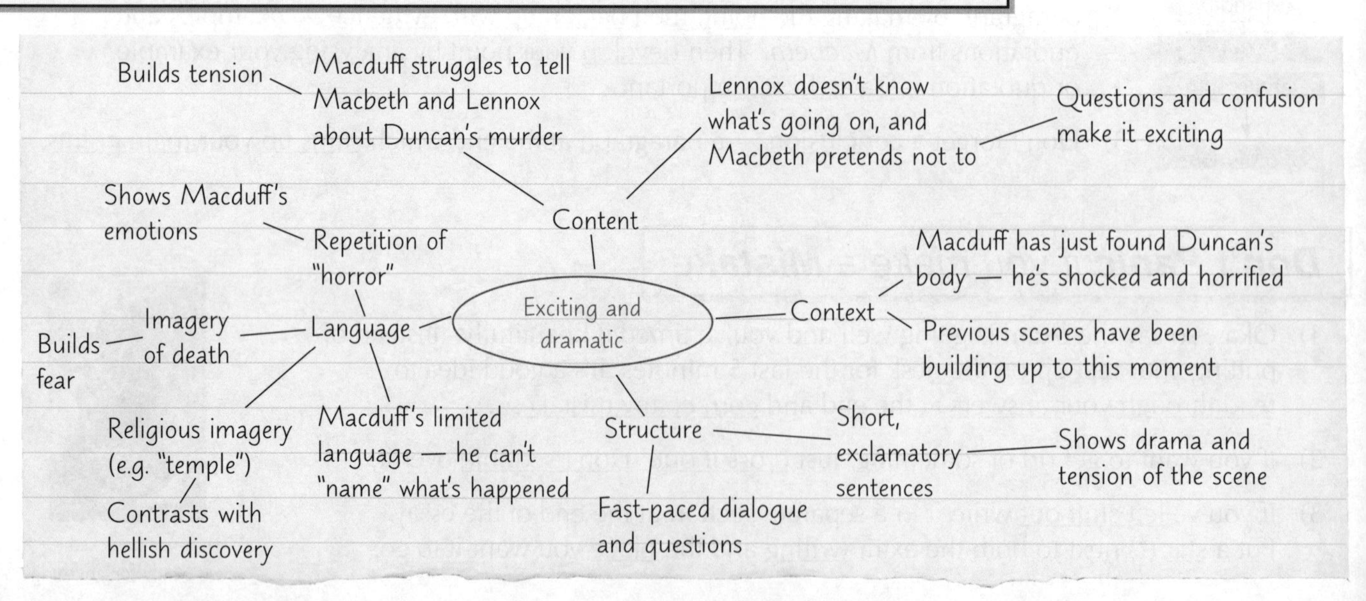

What do examiners eat? Why, egg-sam-wiches of course...

The most important thing to remember is DON'T PANIC. Take a deep breath, read the questions, pick a good 'un, write a plan... take another deep breath... and start writing. Leave five minutes at the end to check your answer too.

Worked Answer

These pages will show you how to write a really impressive answer for Part A, focusing entirely on the extract given in the exam question. You'll need exactly the same skills to answer Part B — the only difference is that for Part B you get to choose which part of the play you write about.

Use your **Introduction** to get off to a **Good Start**

These pages are all about how to word your sentences to impress the examiner, so we haven't included everything from the plan on page 62.

You might start with something like...

> In this extract, Macduff has just discovered Duncan's body, so he is shocked and horrified. The atmosphere of the scene is dramatic and exciting. Macduff's language shows how awful Duncan's death is, and how this has affected him.

1) This intro is okay. It describes what's happened and looks at the atmosphere of the extract.
2) Use the key words from the question to give your essay focus, and to show the examiner you're on track and that you're thinking about the question from the start.
3) But there's still room for improvement — here's a better introduction...

> In this extract, Macduff has just discovered Duncan's body. Shakespeare uses Macduff's language to show how shocked and horrified he is, which makes the scene dramatic and exciting. The "Confusion" and questions from Lennox and Macbeth add to the tension, and provide dramatic irony because the audience knows that Macbeth's "Confusion" is false. As the audience never sees Duncan's body, Shakespeare uses Macduff's reaction to convey how horrific the murder was.

This shows that you're not just describing how Macduff feels, but also focusing on the effect of the language.

This tells the examiner that you've thought about the dramatic purpose of the language.

Develop each point with **Detailed Comments** and **Quotes**

> Macduff's repetition of "horror" emphasises how awful his discovery was. He talks of "great doom" and speaks in short sentences. He uses a lot of exclamations, which makes his language dramatic.

1) This paragraph makes lots of points about the language in this extract. But it doesn't develop the points fully or give details about how the language makes it dramatic and exciting.
2) You should develop your points with detail and comments:

> Macduff's distress at finding Duncan's body is clear from the language he uses. He speaks in short, exclamatory sentences, which makes him sound panicked and upset. This increases the pace of the dialogue and adds to the excitement of the scene. Shakespeare uses exclamations such as "Murder and treason!" to make the language disjointed, which reflects Macduff's thoughts at this moment. He is so shocked by the discovery that he cannot control his speech. This is further highlighted by his statement that "Confusion now hath made his masterpiece" and by Macbeth and Lennox's questions that he cannot answer. When Macduff says "Do not bid me speak", Shakespeare shows Macduff's absolute "horror" at what he has seen. This is reinforced by the repetition of the word "horror", which adds to the drama of the scene.

This makes a relevant point about the extract, and then goes on to comment on the language used.

This develops the point about how Macduff's language shows his state of mind.

Remember to back up your points with quotes from the play.

Referring back to the question keeps your answer focused.

Worked Answer

You need to make a *Variety* of *Points*

Here's a point you could make about the imagery in this extract:

> Shakespeare uses religious imagery to describe King Duncan, as Macduff describes his murder as "sacrilegious". This shows that Duncan was a good king, so his murder was especially immoral.

1) This paragraph introduces the idea that Duncan was a respected monarch.
2) However, you can improve it by discussing how this idea relates to the themes of the play:

> Macduff describes Duncan's murder as "sacrilegious" and portrays Duncan's body as "The Lord's anointed temple". This religious imagery reveals that Macduff had a high opinion of Duncan, and considered him to be a fair and just king. It also corresponds to the idea that a king should be holy, which makes his murder even more dramatic. This impression of Duncan strongly contrasts with Macbeth, who is cruel and immoral. It suggests that he will be a different kind of king to Duncan.

Talking about themes and ideas shows the examiner you're aware of how the extract fits into the play as a whole and how it relates to the audience's ideas at that time.

Don't forget to explain how your points link to the exam question.

3) Don't forget to focus on characterisation — don't treat the characters as real people:

> Shakespeare uses Macduff's distress to reveal his character. Macduff is so loyal to Duncan that he "cannot conceive" that anyone would betray the King. This is the first time that the audience has met Macduff, and Shakespeare introduces him as an honest, decent character. This contrasts with Macbeth, whose appearance of innocence provides dramatic irony, since the audience knows he is a cold-blooded murderer.

Mentioning Shakespeare's techniques shows you're aware that Macduff is a fictional character, and you understand how Shakespeare has used language and other dramatic devices to portray him.

Finish your essay in *Style*

You could say:

> In conclusion, this extract is very exciting and dramatic. Shakespeare uses it to explain to the audience what has happened off-stage, and uses language to make it sound shocking.

1) This conclusion is okay but it doesn't summarise how Shakespeare uses language.
2) So to make it really impressive you could say something like...

> Shakespeare uses Macduff to convey the "horror" of Duncan's murder, using dramatic language and short exclamations to make the scene tense and exciting. Macduff's shock and grief are perhaps more effective than actually showing the murder on stage. Lennox and Macbeth's questions increase the tension, as the audience knows that Macbeth has murdered Duncan. Macbeth's dishonesty adds to the excitement, and the audience is left wondering whether Macbeth's murderous actions will be discovered.

This shows that you've considered the dramatic effect of the scene and are expressing a personal opinion.

Make your last sentence really stand out — it's your last opportunity to impress the examiner.

Why do alligators write good essays — because their quotes are snappy...

It seems like there's a lot to remember on these two pages, but there's not really. To summarise — write a scorching intro and a sizzling conclusion, make a good range of points (one per paragraph) and include plenty of examples. Easy.

Sample Exam — Planning Part B

Phew, now that's over and it's time for a lovely cup of t... oh wait. Fiddlesticks. There's still Part B to answer.

Decide Which Bit of the play to Write about

For Part B you need to show the examiner the same essay-writing skills as for Part A (on pages 63-64). The tricky bit is planning it — you have to choose the passage, so make sure it's a good one.

1) Read the question closely and underline the important bits.

> **Q1 b)** Show how Shakespeare uses language to create an exciting, dramatic atmosphere in another part of the play.

2) Think of all the bits in the play that would be relevant. For example, some dramatic and exciting scenes are: Act 1, Scene 7 (when Macbeth and Lady Macbeth discuss Duncan's murder) and Act 5, Scene 8 (when Macbeth is killed).

3) Have a quick look at the scenes you could write about and pick the one you feel best fits the question — here are some important points to think about:

- Don't choose a really long passage as you won't be able to cover it in enough detail, but it shouldn't be too short either. Just make sure it's long enough for you to write about.
- Make sure the passage can be linked to the themes and ideas of the play.
- The passage should also have interesting bits of structure or language. You'll have a copy of the text in the exam, so there's no excuse not to include some close analysis of the language.

Here's how you could Plan your Answer for Part B

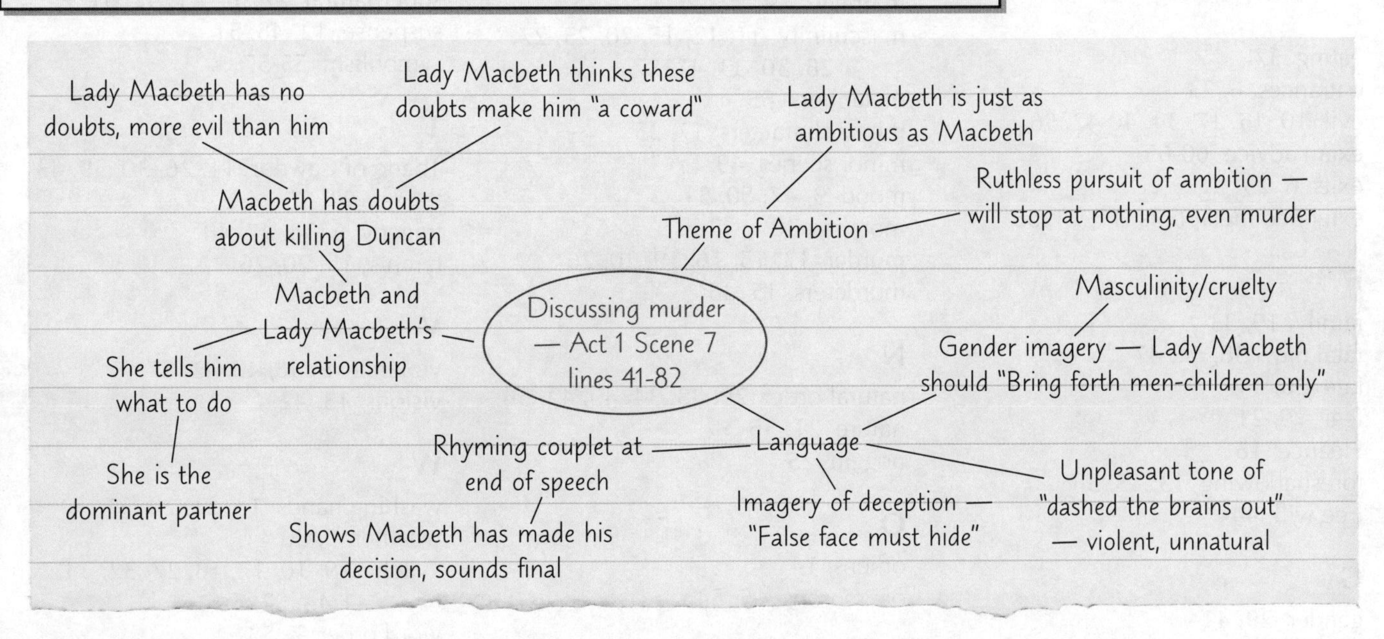

Don't stress about Part B — you might break out in hives...

Keep an eye on the clock, because it's very easy to fritter away precious exam minutes answering Part A perfectly, and neglect Part B. But remember they're worth equal marks — so they need an equal amount of writing time.

Index

The Characters from 'Macbeth'

Phew! You should be an expert on *Macbeth* by now. But if you want a bit of light relief and a quick recap of the play's plot, sit yourself down and read through *Macbeth — The Cartoon*...

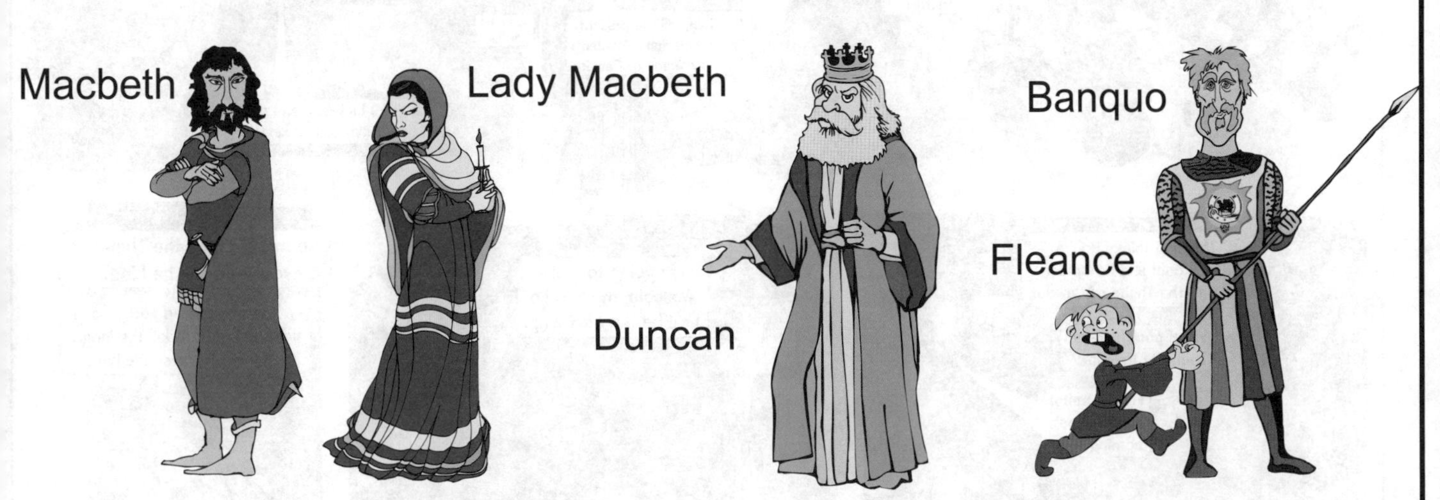

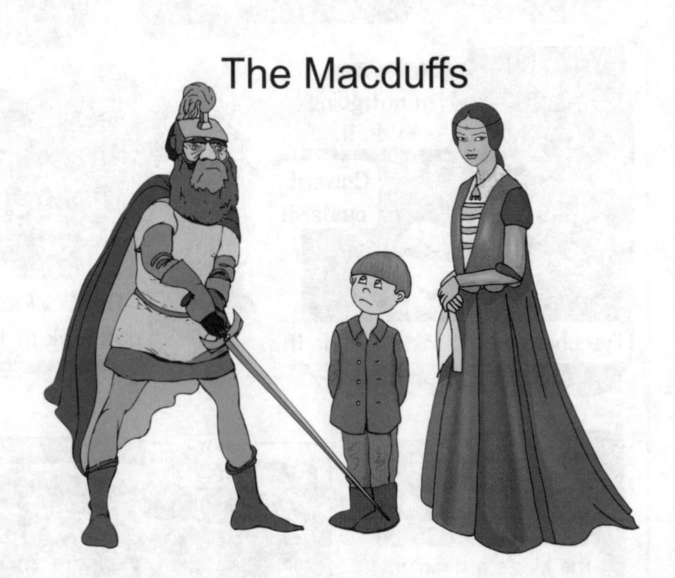

William Shakespeare's 'Macbeth'